Hate Crime

This short, accessible text takes on the global and pervasive phenomenon of hate crimes and hypothesizes potential fixes. Iganski and Levin detail evidence of hate violence in the 21st century, particularly religious hatred, ethnic, racial and xenophobic hatred, violence on the basis of sexual orientation and sexual identity, disablist violence, and violence against women, using the most recently published data from cross-national surveys produced by international organizations. This is an ideal addition to any course on social problems, violence, or hate crimes.

Paul Iganski, Ph.D., is Professor of Criminology and Criminal Justice in the Lancaster University Law School, UK, and a member of the ESRC Centre for Corpus Approaches to Social Science at Lancaster. For a decade-and-a-half he has specialized in research, writing, teaching, and public engagement about hate crime. His books include *Hate Crime and the City*, *Hate Crimes Against London's Jews*, and the edited volumes *Hate Crime: The Consequences of Hate Crime*, and *The Hate Debate*. He mostly conducts his research in collaboration with, or commissioned by, NGOs and the equalities sector in the UK and internationally. At Lancaster University he teaches courses on criminological perspectives on violence, and hate crime, human rights and the State.

Jack Levin, Ph.D., is an Emeritus Professor of Sociology and Criminology and Co-director of the Brudnick Center on Violence and Conflict at Northeastern University, where he teaches courses in the sociology of violence and hate. Levin has authored or co-authored more than 30 books, including *Why We Hate*, *Hate Crimes: The Rising Tide of Bigotry and Bloodshed*, and *The Violence of Hate*. Dr Levin was honored by the Massachusetts Council for Advancement and Support of Education as its "Professor of the Year" and by the American Sociological Association for his contributions to the public understanding of sociology. He has also received awards from the Eastern Sociological Society, Association of Clinical and Applied Sociology, and Society for the Study of Social Problems.

Framing 21st Century Social Issues
Series Editor: France Winddance Twine, University of California–Santa Barbara

The goal of this new, unique series is to offer readable, teachable "thinking frames" on today's social problems and social issues by leading scholars. These are available for view on http://routledge.custom-gateway.com/routledge-social-issues.html.

For instructors teaching a wide range of courses in the social sciences, the Routledge *Social Issues Collection* now offers the best of both worlds: originally written short texts that provide "overviews" to important social issues *as well as* teachable excerpts from larger works previously published by Routledge and other presses.

As an instructor, click to the website to view the library and decide how to build your custom anthology and which thinking frames to assign. Students can choose to receive the assigned materials in print and/or electronic formats at an affordable price.

Available:

The Enduring Color Line in US Athletics
Krystal Beamon and Chris M. Messer

Identity Problems in the Facebook Era
Daniel Trottier

The Pains of Mass Imprisonment
Benjamin Fleury-Steiner and Jamie G. Longazel

From Trafficking to Terror
Constructing a Global Social Problem
Pardis Mahdavi

Unequal Prospects
Is Working Longer the Answer?
Tay McNamara and John Williamson

Beyond the Prison Industrial Complex
Crime and Incarceration in the 21st Century
Kevin Wehr and Elyshia Aseltine

Girls with Guns
Firearms, Feminism, and Militarism
France Winddance Twine

Terror
Social, Political, and Economic Perspectives
Mark Worrell

Torture
A Sociology of Violence and Human Rights
Lisa Hajjar

DIY
The Search for Control and Self-Reliance in the 21st Century
Kevin Wehr

Foreign Remedies
What the Experience of Other Nations Can Tell Us about Next Steps in Reforming US Health Care
David A. Rochefort and Kevin P. Donnelly

Oversharing
Presentation of Self in the Internet Age
Ben Agger

Due Process Denied
Detentions and Deportations in the United States
Tanya Golash-Boza

Disposable Youth
Racialized Memories, and the Culture of Cruelty
Henry Giroux

Nuclear Family Values, Extended Family Lives
The Power of Race, Class, and Gender
Natalia Sarkisian and Naomi Gerstel

How Ethical Systems Change
Lynching and Capital Punishment
Sheldon Ekland-Olson and Danielle Dirks

How Ethical Systems Change
Tolerable Suffering and Assisted Dying
Sheldon Ekland-Olson and Elyshia Aseltine

How Ethical Systems Change
Abortion and Neonatal Care
Sheldon Ekland-Olson and Elyshia Aseltine

How Ethical Systems Change
Eugenics, the Final Solution, Bioethics
Sheldon Ekland-Olson and Julie Beicken

Why Nations Go to War
A Sociology of Military Conflict
Mark P. Worrell

Changing Times for Black Professionals
Adia Harvey Wingfield

Outsourcing the Womb
Race, Class, and Gestational Surrogacy in a Global Market
France Winddance Twine

The Problem of Emotions in Societies
Jonathan H. Turner

Rapid Climate Change
Causes, Consequences, and Solutions
Scott G. McNall

Waste and Consumption
Capitalism, the Environment, and the Life of Things
Simonetta Falasca-Zamponi

The Future of Higher Education
Dan Clawson and Max Page

Contentious Identities
Ethnic, Religious, and Nationalist Conflicts in Today's World
Daniel Chirot

Empire Versus Democracy
The Triumph of Corporate and Military Power
Carl Boggs

The Stupidity Epidemic
Worrying About Students, Schools, and America's Future
Joel Best

Sex, Drugs, and Death
Addressing Youth Problems in American Society
Tammy Anderson

Body Problems
Running and Living Long in a Fast-Food Society
Ben Agger

Hate Crime
A Global Perspective

Paul Iganski and Jack Levin

Routledge
Taylor & Francis Group

NEW YORK AND LONDON

First published 2015
by Routledge
711 Third Avenue, New York, NY 10017

and by Routledge
2 Park Square, Milton Park, Abingdon, Oxon, OX14 4RN

Routledge is an imprint of the Taylor & Francis Group, an informa business

© 2015 Taylor & Francis

Library of Congress Cataloging-in-Publication Data

Iganski, Paul.
   Hate crime : a global perspective / by Paul Iganski and Jack Levin.
      pages cm. — (Framing 21st century social issues)
   Includes bibliographical references and index.
   1. Hate crimes.   I. Title.
   HV6773.5.I327 2015
   364.15—dc23
   2014038775

ISBN: 978-1-138-78954-8 (pbk)
ISBN: 978-1-315-76485-6 (ebk)

Typeset in Adobe GaramondPro
by Apex CoVantage, LLC

Contents

Glossary   ix

Preface: Hate Crime: A Global Phenomenon   xiii

1. Religious Hatred   1

2. Racial, Ethnic, and Xenophobic Violence   8

3. Homophobic and Transphobic Violence   17

4. Disablist Violence   23

5. Violence against Women   28

6. The Brutality of Hate   35

7. A Typology of the Motives of Hate Crime Offenders   43

8. Hate Violence and Emotion   52

9. Changing Cultures: Challenging Hate   58

References   64

Index   70

Glossary

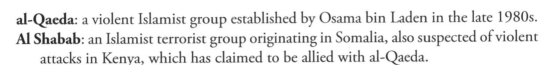

al-Qaeda: a violent Islamist group established by Osama bin Laden in the late 1980s.

Al Shabab: an Islamist terrorist group originating in Somalia, also suspected of violent attacks in Kenya, which has claimed to be allied with al-Qaeda.

caliphate: an Islamic political and religious state. Historically, an empire from the 7th to the 13th centuries, at times covering southwest Asia, the Middle East, North Africa, and Spain.

Council of Europe: an independent international organization headquartered in Strasbourg with membership from 47 countries in Europe, established to promote democracy and protect human rights and the rule of law in Europe (see: http://www.coe.int/en/).

Crusades: a series of expeditionary wars under the banner of Christianity from 1096 to the latter 13th century, undertaken to recapture the Holy Land and other parts of the Middle East from Muslim domination.

disablist: manifesting discrimination, hostility, or prejudice against people with disabilities.

ethnic cleansing: actions to create ethnically or religiously homogeneous territory by terrorizing and forcibly displacing people from particular ethnic or religious communities.

European Commission against Racism and Intolerance: a human rights body of the Council of Europe consisting of independent experts, established to monitor and report on racial, ethnic, and xenophobic intolerance and discrimination (see: http://www.coe.int/t/dghl/monitoring/ecri/default_en.asp).

European Union Agency for Fundamental Rights: a decentralized agency of the European Union established to provide expert advice to EU institutions and Member States concerning fundamental rights, discrimination, and access to justice (see: http://fra.europa.eu/en).

European Union Minorities and Discrimination Survey: undertaken by the European Union Agency for Fundamental Rights in 2008, the first survey to systematically interview face-to-face minority ethnic and religious groups in all European Union Member States.

Golden Dawn: a Greek nationalist movement and political party that employs Nazi-like symbolism in its emblems.

hate crime: hate violence against persons or property that is criminalized and subject to greater penalties than otherwise identical crimes where denigration of perceived social identity plays no part.

hate violence: violence in which the denigration of a person's perceived identity, such as their race, their ethnicity, gender, religion, sexual orientation, disability status, or sexual orientation or identity, plays some role in the violent act.

Inquisition: a judicial process and institutions established by the Roman Catholic Church between the 12th and early 19th centuries to root out, combat, and punish heresy among followers.

Islamic State of Iraq and Syria (ISIS): the last S of ISIS is from the Arabic word *al-Sham*, which, depending on the context, is used to refer to the Levant (a historical geographical collective term for the countries bordering the eastern Mediterranean), or alternatively Syria. ISIS is also known as the Islamic State of Iraq and the Levant (ISIL), or just the Islamic State, and it is sometimes referred to as DAESH, an acronym that takes the first letters of the Arabic words for ISIS. An offshoot of al-Qaeda, ISIS is a violent Islamist movement seeking to create an extremist version of a Sunni Islamic state.

Jihads: often understood to refer to Holy Wars. But literally, Jihad means "struggle" or "effort" to faithfully follow the Muslim faith, construct a good Muslim society, or defend Islam by force if necessary.

Ku Klux Klan: different social movements in the United States, some historically associated with secrecy, cross burnings, and violence against African Americans.

National Coalition of Anti-Violence Programs: a national organization in the United States that aims to reduce violence and its consequences as experienced by lesbian, gay, bisexual, and transgender persons (see: http://www.ncavp.org/).

New Scotland Yard: the headquarters of London's Metropolitan Police Service.

Office for Democratic Institutions and Human Rights: an institution of the Organization for Security and Co-operation in Europe established in 1991 to promote democratic elections and respect for human rights, non-discrimination, and the rule of law (see: http://www.osce.org/odihr).

queer: originally used as a pejorative term referring to lesbian, gay, bisexual, and transgender people it has now been appropriated by some LGBT persons as a bonding term of community identification. It is still highly offensive, however, when used as an epithet or as a term of disparagement of a person's sexual orientation or sexual identity.

Racist Violence Recording Network: a network set up in Greece in 2011 by the Office for the United Nations Commissioner for Refugees (UNHCR) in cooperation with the Greek National Commission for Human Rights, NGOs, and grassroots movements to systematically record and monitor racist violence in Greece.

Rigby, Lee (Corporal): a British Army soldier who was stabbed and hacked to death on a south London street while off duty on May 22, 2013, by two attackers who told witnesses that they were avenging the killing of Muslims by British armed forces.

sectarian: acts of hostility between different denominations of a religion.

South African Human Rights Commission: a national institution established in South Africa in 1995 to support constitutional democracy and defend human rights (see: http://www.sahrc.org.za/home/).

Southern Poverty Law Center (SPLC): founded in 1971 by civil rights lawyers Morris Dees and Joseph Levin Jr., the SPLC fights hate and bigotry through litigation, education, and advocacy, and also monitors hate groups and extremists in the United States (see: http://www.splcenter.org/).

UNICEF: the United Nations Children's Fund, a program and organization established in 1946 to promote and protect the rights and welfare of children (see: http://www.unicef.org/).

Western World: countries of the Western hemisphere (including the United States and former European colonies in South America), beyond the Western hemisphere (including European countries and formerly non-Communist Eastern Europe), and Oceania countries (including Australia and New Zealand). All are associated historically with Greco-Roman civilization and Christianity, or their export through colonialism.

World Health Organization: an agency of the United Nations established in 1948 to provide global leadership and coordination on health matters (see: http://www.who.int/en/).

xenophobic: fear of, or hostility and prejudice toward, those perceived to be from different countries or cultures.

Yazidi: a religion, with adherents residing primarily in parts of Iraq, Iran, Syria, Turkey, and the Caucasus region.

Preface
Hate Crime: A Global Phenomenon

Sadly, **hate violence** is a global phenomenon. It occurs in nations in all regions of the world—in states which have different cultural traditions, colonial and post-colonial histories, diverse religious traditions, varieties of political systems, and a broad range of economies. Although the particular contexts for acts of hate violence may differ from country to country and even within individual countries, what is striking is its persistence.

Despite the diversity of nations, hate violence is definitely a universal problem. If it is conceived as violence in which the denigration of a person's perceived identity, such as their 'race,' their ethnicity, gender, religion, sexual orientation, disability status, or sexual identity plays some role, then hate violence can be found in every known society on earth. If it is conceived not only in terms of direct physical acts but also as 'violence of the word,' to use a phrase coined some years ago to characterize threats, slurs, epithets, and other forms of verbal denigration and hateful invective (Matsuda 1989: 2332), then hate violence has always prevailed throughout human existence.

This is not to suggest that the degree of hate violence is a constant in human existence, because it isn't. On the contrary, there have been places and times in which peace and respect for differences vastly overruled the presence of hate, and inter-group relations were marked by peace and tranquility rather than warfare. At the other extreme, there have also been places and times in human history when hate violence overwhelmed all efforts to eradicate it, causing tremendous harm and damage to be initiated and maintained between groups.

Yet the recognition that hate violence deserves to have—given its potentially devastating impact on individuals, communities, and inter-group relations—is far from universal. While it is true that acts of direct physical violence are criminalized in all nations, and in some nations forms of verbal violence are criminalized too, in only a few nations is hate violence legally defined and outlawed as '**hate crime**.' Hence, in this book we use the terms 'hate violence' and 'hate crime' interchangeably. At the same time, we operate under the assumption that criminal acts of hate operate to replace civility and peace with hostility and conflict, and that the world would be a much better place for human affairs if hate violence were to be reduced to a minimum.

Different countries cannot even agree upon the phenomenon to which hate crime refers. The nearest to what might be considered a universal definition of hate crime is provided by the **Office for Democratic Institutions and Human Rights** (ODIHR) of the Organization for Security and Co-Operation in Europe—a security-focused intergovernmental organization with 57 participating countries spanning Europe, central Asia and North America. ODIHR defines a hate crime as a criminal act committed with bias motives, that is, an offense motivated by intolerance toward a certain socially defined group, in that the "perpetrator intentionally chose the target of the crime because of some *protected characteristic*": 'race,' religion, ethnicity, language, or sexual orientation (ODIHR 2009: 16). While this definition captures the essence of what we regard as hate crime and accounts for most types of hate crime offenses, its focus on hate crime as targeted crime does not seem to account for the numerous incidents of hate violence in which the victim is not specifically targeted in a premeditated act of hate, and where instead the 'hate' is peripheral to the crime or it surfaces as an inter-personal conflict escalates—as we discuss in Chapter 8 of this book when focusing on the motivating impulses behind hate crime.

Given the concise length of the book—aimed at making it accessible for both the academic and general reader—it is not our goal to offer a sustained analysis of the problem of hate violence in any particular countries. We do provide snapshots of some countries where there are particularly egregious problems of hate violence but mostly focus on cross-national patterns and themes. The common occurrence of hate violence across nations suggests commonalities of human behavior beyond any specific national context. It is these commonalities of violence against persons because of some aspect of their social identity that is the focus of this book.

To date, research and scholarship on the problem of hate crime has focused primarily on North America—where the labeling of particular types of crime as 'hate crime' began in the United States in the 1970s and then more recently in the 21st century in Europe, primarily in the UK. These are the two parts of the world where the authors of this book reside and work. However, our goal is to offer a global perspective on hate violence by taking some steps to move beyond the US- and UK-centric research and provide analytic observations about hate violence that can only be made from a comparative cross-national viewpoint. Where we can, we draw upon the most recently published data from cross-national surveys produced by international organizations. Moreover, we are not shy about making suggestions, based on our decades of experience studying the phenomenon, regarding the reduction of hate violence.

Our primary objective involves taking what is a relatively new direction in the literature by documenting hate crime as a truly global phenomenon. The first half of the book provides a whirlwind round-the-world tour of some of the evidence of hate violence in the 21st century and its impact and consequences, including religious hatred; ethnic, racial, and xenophobic hatred; violence on the basis of sexual orientation and sexual identity; disablist violence; and violence against women. These are the various forms of violence that we firmly frame as hate crime.

We not only document the problem of hate violence around the world: we also provide some analytic observations and draw out key patterns. The attention we give to religious hatred importantly begins to redress a general neglect of the issue in the hate crimes literature, given that religious bigotry is possibly the most dominant force that frames hate violence to date globally in the 21st century. And in discussing the impact and consequences of hate violence, we show that it is a discriminatory version of violence that can be more egregious than other forms of destructive criminal behavior. That is why hate violence is singled out for particular concern by this book.

For all types of hate crime, we argue that there is a common denominator which involves a cultural basis—a widespread denigration of persons to one degree or another across diverse nations and communities which permits discrimination, oppression and violence. In taking some steps beyond what has been called a "silo approach" to identity (Mason-Bish 2015)—a concern with a single aspect of a person's identity as the focus of hate crime victimization—we also provide some insights into how some social identities intersect in the victimization characteristic of some types of hate violence. However, we also argue that insights about the cultural foundations in which hate violence is nested provide a necessary but still insufficient understanding of hate crime. Specifically, a cultural analysis by itself does not explain why some people offend and why many others who live in the same cultural milieu do not. We turn to this vexing question in the second half of the book in Chapters 7 and 8 where we offer insights into the motivating impulses behind hate violence to explore more precisely the relationship between the background cultures of denigration and the foreground acts of hate violence. We argue that there are certain benefits of expressing hate violence, from the perpetrator's viewpoint, that must be considered in order to understand why victims are chosen for abusive behavior. Hate exists, but it exists in the context of various motivations to strike out for the purpose of being protective of privilege, securing bragging rights with friends, feeling a sense of power, and maintaining an important membership with likeminded bigots.

In some instances, hate violence is also an expression of grievances shared by many others apart from the perpetrator, and the victim of hate violence provides a convenient scapegoat for those grievances. Hate violence is also triggered in emotionally charged situations, often where the person who becomes the perpetrator of hate violence feels that they themselves have been wronged or disrespected. While we are not the first to focus on the role that emotion plays in hate violence, the thinking that we offer arguably takes the hate crimes literature some steps further in exploring emotion in the impulses behind hate-motivated offenses.

Overall, our aims are to encourage the college student reader, and other readers as well, to think critically about key themes and issues in the occurrence and causes of hate crime by applying a cross-national perspective. We also hope to encourage students to apply this global perspective for the purpose of thinking critically about the relationship between the background cultural foundations of hate violence and the foreground of particular acts of hate crime and, at the same time, to consider in a critical light the range of appropriate interventions to manage and prevent hate crime.

We would like to thank the series editor France Winddance Twine for her encouragement and support for this book. At Routledge, we are grateful to Steve Rutter and Margaret Moore for their guidance throughout the course of producing our manuscript. We also owe a debt of gratitude to the following reviewers and colleagues whose feedback contributed to improvements in the final version: Stephanie Cappadona, Curry College; Carolyn Petrosino, Bridgewater State University; Katie Swope, Stevenson University; and Peter Grant.

Paul Iganski, Lancaster University
Jack Levin, Northeastern University

1:   Religious Hatred

Violence in the name of religion has a long and bloody history. Islamic **Jihads** from the 7th century, the **Crusades** in the 11th–13th centuries, the **Inquisition** from the 13th–19th centuries, claimed thousands upon thousands of lives for religion. And in the 21st century, when viewed from a global perspective, religious bigotry is a dominant—and possibly even the foremost—force framing hate violence. As we will illuminate in this chapter, however, there is no singular role that religion plays in the experience of hate violence: in some instances it is the main impetus, in others it is only peripheral.

The 21st century dawned with an extreme act of hate violence: the September 11, 2001, **al-Qaeda** terror attacks on the World Trade Center, in rural Pennsylvania, and against the Pentagon in the United States. The intended targets were symbols of secular political, economic, and military might (Juergensmeyer 2003: 61). The casualties were the nearly 3,000 people, mostly civilians, who lost their lives in a horrible conflagration. The acts combined religious conviction, loathing of secular society, and hatred of the United States. They were nourished by a tradition of radical Islamic political ideology justifying the wielding of violence against those deemed to be hostile to Islam (Juergensmeyer 2003: 80–84). In return, scapegoating against those perceived to be Arab or Muslim followed in the United States with a huge spike in violence and discrimination accompanied by public expressions of vitriol about Islam by certain elected politicians and evangelicals (Welch 2006: 62–76). For a period of time, anyone who had dark skin and spoke with an accent—those who might possibly have come from a Middle Eastern country—was at increased risk for victimization.

After that ominous preface to the 21st century, the state of affairs concerning religious violence just worsened in different parts of the world. The Minority Rights Group International—a campaigning non-governmental organization founded in the 1970s to defend the rights of disadvantaged minorities and indigenous people—has been compiling annually since 2005 the Peoples under Threat index, ranking countries at greatest risk of genocide, mass killing or other systematic violent repression. In many instances, the threat manifests itself as religious, **sectarian**, or ethnic conflict and persecution. In some instances, the religious, sectarian, and ethnic dynamics of the conflicts are entangled in a complex web of forces behind violence.

Middle East and African states dominate as those with peoples most at risk of mass killing. Eight countries—including Somalia, Sudan, Democratic Republic of Congo, Afghanistan, Iraq, Pakistan, Myanmar (formerly Burma) and Ethiopia—have consistently ranked each year in the top ten at greatest risk. Each year, Somalia has been ranked as the highest risk, and since 2010, Sudan has been ranked in second place, rising from third in 2008 and 2009. A few other countries have featured intermittently in the top ten at greatest risk: Chad (2010), Côte d'Ivoire (2011), Iran (2012), Israel/Palestine (2009), Nigeria (2013), South Sudan (2012), Syria (2013 & 2014) and Yemen (2014). Religious and sectarian conflicts feature prominently in a number of these countries.

Extreme Islamist Violence

Syria's entry into the top ten rankings in 2013 and its rise to the third-ranked country most at risk of genocide, mass killing, or other forms of mass oppression has been associated with the increasingly sectarian complexion (Lattimer 2014) of the devastating civil war besetting the country. Islamist militias with a sectarian agenda perpetrate atrocities propelled by religious zealotry. One such group, the **Islamic State of Iraq and Syria (ISIS)**—an offshoot of al-Qaeda—extended its reach by sweeping through neighboring Iraq in 2014. Its actions attracted volunteer recruits from Muslim communities around the world including Europe, the Caucasus, the United States, and Arab countries. ISIS slickly used social media, apps, and even a Hollywood-style feature-length movie to attract new recruits, spread its message, and intimidate enemies. By late 2014 ISIS was in control of a large swath of territory spanning across Syria and Iraq, and its goal was to reach much further by establishing an Islamic **caliphate** from the Middle East, North Africa, large areas of Asia, and including the Balkans, Austria, and Spain in Europe.

Islam has two major denominations: Sunni and Shi'a. While there are numerous forces—historical, geo-political, and economic—responsible for hatching and incubating the violence in Syria and Iraq, extremist Sunni Muslim religious ideology has also played a central role in attacks against Shi'a. The violence has not only been sectarian in nature. Ideologically and theologically incited violence was also targeted at Iraqi Christians. In July 2014, the international news media widely reported that Christians had begun fleeing the Iraqi city of Mosul after ISIS issued a threat that they would be killed unless they converted to Islam or paid a protection tax called a "jizya." A similar ultimatum to Christians had been issued in the Syrian city of Raqqa a few months earlier.

In further episodes of violence widely reported by the international news media in August 2014, Islamic State extremists allegedly slaughtered hundreds of Iraq's **Yazidi** ethnic and religious minority community in and around the village of Kocho in northern Iraq. The Islamic State fighters reportedly demanded that the Yazidis convert to Islam or face death. After refusing to convert, the ensuing violence was not only impelled by religious bigotry, but also gendered in character. Men were slaughtered. Women and children abducted: the women carried off into sexual servitude and slavery.

By the summer of 2014, fleeing from the advances of ISIS in northern Iraq, hundreds of thousands of displaced Iraqis from minority communities, not only Yazidis, were seeking refuge near the Turkish border. The international news media widely reported the humanitarian crisis facing tens of thousands of Yazidis trapped in harrowing conditions and exposed to a hostile climate of soaring temperatures after fleeing to Mount Sinjar. Air drops of humanitarian aid including water and shelter were made by the US, UK, and Iraqi air forces.

Sectarian Violence

Elsewhere, violent attacks against Shi'a Muslims have been on the rise in Pakistan since the 1980s (Mihlar 2014). In 2013 alone there were an estimated 700 targeted killings of Shi'a, mostly perpetrated by extremist Sunni groups. The most active Sunni militant groups include Lashkar-e-Jhangri (LeJ), Sipah-e-Sahaba Pakistan (SSP) and Tehrik-e-Taliban Pakistan (TTP), which subscribe to and promote an extreme Sunni Islamic ideology in which Shi'a Muslims are denigrated as heretics, apostates, infidels, impure, and unclean, and their killing religiously justified. Shi'a have been vilified and denigrated in Pakistan in campaigns of hate speech in mosques, schools, and social media. The roots of the violence are not only religious, as there is a cauldron of geo-political, social, ethnic, and religious forces at work in which ethnic Hazara Shi'a Muslims in Pakistan's south western region of Balochistan have borne the brunt of the violence.

In a particularly notorious attack near the town of Mastung in 2011, a bus on its way to visit holy sites in Iran was forced off the road by gunmen who separated out the Hazara Shi'as from the Sunni passengers, killed 26 Shi'as and wounded six others, and let the Sunnis go. In another notorious attack in 2013, coordinated suicide bomb attacks on a snooker club in Quetta claimed the lives of 96 Hazaras and wounded 150 others.

Religious and sectarian violence has also been severe in Myanmar (formerly Burma)—another of the countries ranked by the Minority Rights Group International in the top ten at greatest risk of genocide, mass killing, or other systematic violent repression. In June and October 2012, sectarian violence between ethnic Arakanese Buddhists and Rohingya Muslims in Arakan state, Myanmar, claimed the lives of 211 people according to the Myanmar government, while Human Rights Watch estimated many more (Human Rights Watch 2013).

There is a long history of violence between Buddhists and Muslims in Arakan State stretching back over decades. And while both populations have faced past oppression by Myanmar governments, the Rohingya population, which is denied citizenship and considered by many to be illegal immigrants, has particularly faced routine persecution and forcible displacement. The outbreak of violence in June 2012 was triggered in late May by the rape and murder of an Arakanese woman in Ramri Township by three Muslim men. Arakanese villagers retaliated by stopping a bus southeast of Ramri and killed 10 Muslim passengers. Communal violence then escalated. Allegedly, state security forces initially stood by without intervening to halt the violence, and later joined Arakanese mobs in attacking and burning Muslim villages and neighborhoods (Human Rights Watch 2013: 7).

In further violence in October 2012, Muslim villages in nine townships across Arakan State were attacked by Arakanese men armed with swords, machetes, homemade firearms, and Molotov cocktails. Again, security forces allegedly either stood by or participated in the violence. Further outbreaks of violence against Muslims in 2013, which spread beyond Arakan State to other parts of Myanmar, claimed more lives with numerous homes burnt to the ground.

In the two years following the outbreak of this latest round of inter-communal violence in Myanmar, the United Nations Commission for Human Rights estimated that 87,000 people had departed irregularly by sea from the Bangladesh-Myanmar border region heading for Thailand, Malaysia, Indonesia, and Australia (UNHCR 2014). Many were transported by smugglers in cramped conditions and subjected to verbal and physical abuse. Hundreds reportedly died from the deprivations of the journey and violence by smugglers. Some drowned while trying to escape in desperation (UNHCR 2014). Bangladesh closed its borders, returning Rohingya asylum seekers to sea. Thailand also resisted the influx of asylum seekers (Human Rights Watch 2013: 16).

Elsewhere in the region, in September 2013, communal violence between Hindu Jat and Muslim communities in the Muzaffarnagar and Shamli districts of Uttar Pradesh in India left at least 65 people dead and many injured. Numerous homes in villages were burnt to the ground and 50,000 people were reportedly displaced by the conflict (Hassan 2014). The violence occurred in the context of regular incidents of inter-communal violence and the sewing of communal hostilities by political parties and was stoked by hate speech and incitement in print and social media, escalating a number of trigger incidents (Hassan 2014).

Violence against Muslims in the Western World

The 9/11 terror attacks in the United States in 2001 triggered a wave of anti-Muslim incidents across the **Western World**. In Europe, the then European Monitoring

Centre on Racism and Xenophobia (EUMC) (now the **European Union Agency for Fundamental Rights** [FRA]), proposed that the 9/11 attacks triggered a latent Islamophobia—a widespread fear and loathing of Muslims. And even though physical attacks against Muslims generally seemed small in number, verbal abuse in person, and abuse by phone or by email to Muslim organizations was widely reported in most countries (EUMC 2001). Muslim women, especially, were targeted. Mosques and Islamic cultural centers were also targeted in acts of vandalism and desecration (Allen & Nielsen 2002: 7).

A few years later, reflecting back on events following 9/11 in Britain, a report by the Commission on British Muslims and Islamophobia noted that "Thousands of British Muslims have tales to tell from the days after 9/11—rudeness and insensitivity, or worse, from colleagues, associates and neighbors, and from total strangers in shops and buses, trains and streets" (Commission on British Muslims and Islamophobia 2004:16).

The continuing nature of anti-Muslim victimization across the early 21st century was revealed recently by the 2008 EU-MIDIS survey—which interviewed Muslim respondents in fourteen EU Member States (FRA 2009a). Just over one in ten (11 percent) Muslim respondents, in the fourteen states combined, reported at least one incident of personal racist criminal victimization—including assaults, threats, and serious harassment—during the previous twelve months. Many experienced more than one incident, and the average for Muslim victims of personal racist crime was three incidents in the previous 12 months.

Notably, the majority of victims did not report their experience to the police, some suggesting that they were too trivial or not worth reporting—possibly indicating the normalization of incidents. Others lacked confidence in the police being able to do anything. And it is likely that some were reticent about involving the police, given the targeting of Muslims in the 'War on Terror' in a number of European countries following the 9/11 attacks.

In addition to the routine victimization of Muslims, waves of anti-Muslim violence in some countries have been triggered by further extreme events since 9/11:

- In 2004 in the Netherlands in the days after the murder of the film maker Theo van Gogh, who was assassinated by a radicalized young Muslim, there was reportedly an outbreak of incidents, including assaults, arson attacks, and criminal damage of mosques and Islamic schools (Veldhuis & Bakker 2009: 25).
- A backlash of attacks against Muslims in London and elsewhere in Britain occurred following the 2005 London bombings.
- A further spike in anti-Muslim attacks followed the murder of **Corporal Lee Rigby** on a South London street in 2013.

Understanding the Relationship between Religion and Hate Violence

Jonathan Swift, the 17th–18th century Anglo-Irish satirist, essayist, poet, and cleric, and author of *Gulliver's Travels*, in commenting on centuries of bloodshed in the name of religion, famously wrote that "We have just enough religion to make us hate, but not enough to make us love one another" (Haught 1990: 12). Yet, as the examples in this chapter indicate, there is no singular role that religion plays in hate violence.

In the instances of violence we have covered, there are three major ways in which religion is implicated. First, theologically-driven hate characterizes some of the atrocities committed by radical groups such as ISIS in Iraq. Based on a long history of theological documentation, members of other denominations or religious groups are seen as sub-humans, infidels, or children of the devil who deserve to be wiped from the face of the earth. The dehumanization of outsiders facilitates the commission of inhumane and brutal acts of violence—for example, distributing videos in which westerners are beheaded by a masked ISIS leader.

Second, inter-communal, or sectarian, hatreds characterize the violence between Sunni and Shi'a Muslims in Pakistan, Buddhists and Muslims in Myanmar, and Hindu Jat and Muslim communities in the Muzaffarnagar and Shamli districts of Uttar Pradesh in India. However, while sectarian violence coalesces around religious identity, religion is not often the primary driving force behind such violence. Take Pakistan, for instance: the Sunni-Shi'a violence has deep historical roots stretching back at least to the 1947 partition of colonial India and the resultant migration of communities in the Pakistani Punjab. Economic and social deprivations suffered by Sunni rural laboring communities in South Punjab were transformed by political agitation into sectarian hatred against Shi'a who were dominant among the land-owning classes and the urban elites. Later, Islamization policies, theologically in step with the majority Sunni population and promoted by Pakistan's government in the 1980s, met with Shi'a resistance. Regional conflicts exacerbated these sectarian tensions. The newly formed Islamic Republic of Iran sponsored Shi'a activism. And in Pakistan during the Iran-Iraq war in the 1980s, Shi'a sectarian groups which sided with Iran, and Sunni sectarian groups which sided with Iraq, fought a proxy war. Cycles of violence resulted in growing radicalization and further sectarian division (Grare 2007).

Third, in the case of violence against Muslims in the West, religious animosity plays a peripheral role in the violence. Muslims are victimized because of their religious identity. But attacks are not theologically driven. They occur for other reasons, essentially having nothing to do with religion: primarily, the scapegoating of Muslims for extremist Islamist terror attacks. A snapshot listed by Perry (2003) of retaliatory attacks against Muslims in the United States following the 9/11 attacks, for example, shows little evidence of sentiments defaming Islam as a faith or attacking the tenets of Islamic teaching. Instead, the motivation for the attacks is some visceral conception of Muslims—essentially an equation between all Muslims and terrorists, suicide bombers, al-Qaeda, and bin-Laden. This is entangled with **xenophobic** hostility against Muslims as 'outsiders.'

While we have covered in this chapter three major ways in which religion is implicated in hate violence, there will be further variations evident in instances of violence that we haven't had space to include. By the same token, numerous other determinants of violence interacting with religious hatred and divisions, beyond the examples we have provided in this chapter, could be deduced. However, the fundamental point that we have tried to make in taking a global perspective is that while religion is implicated in much hate violence, and violence involving religious hatred to some degree or another has perhaps been the dominant form of hate violence globally so far in the 21st century, religion is rarely the sole determinant. While in this chapter we have tried to pull out the threads of religion involved in the patchwork of variables that interact and result in hate violence, in the next chapter we turn to other determinants: the racial, ethnic, and xenophobic complexion of hate violence.

QUESTIONS FOR DISCUSSION

1. What role does religion play in hate violence in the 21st century?
2. Do conflicts over religious differences primarily fuel sectarian violence?
3. If religious hostility is seen to aggravate victimization of Muslims in the West, what are the other forces at work impelling the violence?

2: Racial, Ethnic, and Xenophobic Violence

~~~

While religious hatred has featured prominently among incidents of hate violence in regions of conflict in the Middle East, South Asia, and Africa, and in other more stable nations, racial, ethnic, and xenophobic violence is also a global problem. In the Western world, it is arguably one of the most dominant forms of hate violence.

There is a long history of racist violence in the United States, beginning with brutal warfare between early settlers and Native Americans. During the 18th and 19th centuries, black Americans were caught in a legal system of slavery which eventually covered all of the states located below the so-called Mason-Dixon line. During a brief period known as reconstruction following the end of the Civil War, murders of newly freed slaves escalated. Black Americans were, for the first time, given an opportunity to amass power and wealth, a condition that certain white Americans would not tolerate. Into the 20th century, former Confederate officers joined together in a white supremacist organization known as the **Ku Klux Klan** which came to burn crosses and then lynch former slaves who had become competitive with whites for status, power, and economic resources. By the 1920s, the Klan had increased its membership to some 4 million members and had expanded its acrimony beyond race to encompass Catholics and Jews. Until civil rights laws were passed during the 1960s, black Americans continued to be second-class citizens who, under a legal system of segregation known as Jim Crow, were victims of institutionalized discrimination and violence.

The problem of violence based on racial differences continues into the 21st century. Nationwide hate crime data annually published on the FBI's Uniform Crime Reports (UCR) web pages show that, in over half of the offenses recorded each year, the victims were targeted because of their race or ethnicity. A majority involve bias-motivated attacks against African-Americans and other people of color (see Figure 2.1).

It is very well known though that crimes recorded by law enforcement agencies are an unreliable indicator of the true extent of criminal behavior. For a variety of reasons, many victims do not report crimes to the police—and the police do not record all offenses reported to them. Because of the limitations of police-recorded crime data, a number of nations use victimization surveys to more accurately estimate the prevalence of crime.

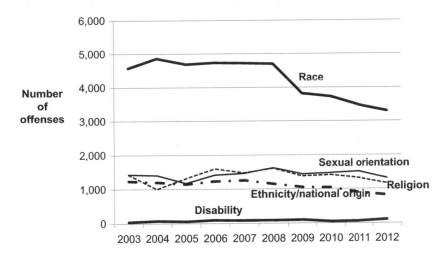

Figure 2.1 FBI hate crime statistics offenses by bias motivation 2003–2012.

Source: United States Department of Justice, Federal Bureau of Investigation, Crime Statistics, Uniform Crime Reports, Hate Crime Statistics http://www.fbi.gov/stats-services/crimestats

In the US, more reliable annual estimates of hate crime based on the National Crime Victimization Survey (NCVS) swamp the FBI's Uniform Crime Reports figures:

- Just over a quarter of a million hate crime victimizations annually against persons aged 12 and over were estimated for the years 2007–2011 by the NCVS—approximately 30 times more than the FBI's UCR figures.
- Furthermore, while the number of hate crime victimizations captured in the UCR data shows a decline over the recent decade by about 15 percent between 2003 and 2012, the NCVS annual estimates remained stable. What the NCVS does show is a decline in the reporting of hate crimes to the police: a drop from 46 percent of victimizations in the survey reported to the police in 2003–2006 to 35 percent in 2007–2011.
- The NCVS also indicates a similar rate of violent victimization on the basis of racial bias: Hispanic, white, and black/African American respondents experienced similar rates of violent victimization for the years 2007–2011—another finding at odds with the UCR data (Sandholtz et al. 2013).

In looking elsewhere in the Western World, a reliable comparative account of the problem of racial, ethnic, and xenophobic violence was provided by the first ever, and to date the only, cross-national survey to specifically sample immigrants and people from minority ethnic communities in Europe—the **European Union Minorities and Discrimination Survey (EU-MIDIS)**—which was carried out in 2008 (FRA 2012). Across the European Union, 23,500 people from immigrant and minority ethnic communities were interviewed about their perceived experiences with discrimination and criminal victimization. A comparative sample of 5,000 people from the majority population living in the same areas as the minorities was also interviewed.

The survey showed that the more visible respondents were in respect of their minority identity, the more likely they were on average to report experiencing criminal victimization in general. At the same time, though, the experience of victimization within the same minority groups differed depending upon the country in which they lived.

Roma/Gypsy communities reported the highest levels of racist victimization. Five hundred Roma respondents were interviewed in each of seven EU Member States—Bulgaria, Czech Republic, Greece, Hungary, Poland, Romania, and Slovakia—in 2008. In each of these countries, the Roma were the most victimized minority group surveyed—along with Sub-Saharan Africans.

Almost a fifth (18 percent) of Roma respondents in the survey reported at least one incident of personal racist criminal victimization—including assaults, threats, and serious harassment—in the last twelve months (FRA 2009b: 65). The rates of reported racist victimization of Roma ranged from 32 percent of Roma respondents in Czechoslovakia—the highest rate of victimization for any group surveyed in any country—to 26 percent in Greece and Poland, to 3 percent in Bulgaria.

Extremist Violence in Europe

In some European countries, extremism, as a determinant of hate violence, appears to be on the rise. The Council of Europe's **European Commission against Racism and Intolerance (ECRI)** noted in its annual report for 2013 growing support for nationalist, xenophobic, and neo-Nazi political parties (ECRI 2014: 7).

Particular concern about Greece and Hungary was noted in 2013 by the **European Union Fundamental Rights Agency** (FRA). These two countries stand out from many other European countries in that both have experienced severe economic deprivation in recent years, and in both countries far-right parties espousing anti-minority and anti-immigrant rhetoric have gained significant footholds in national parliaments. The hostile climates heated by extremist politics have produced environments particularly conducive to race hate crime.

Among EU Member States, Greece has probably suffered most from the global financial crisis and the Eurozone debt crisis of recent years. In 2013, more than half of under-25-year-olds were unemployed in Greece: more than twice the level of the already high overall unemployment rate of 27 percent. As well as the financial burdens arising from job losses, Greeks have been straining under the burden of pay cuts, tax hikes, public sector financial retrenchment, and cut-backs. Combined with these economic deprivations, by the start of 2010, Greece had also become the main gateway for entry into Europe, especially by those fleeing the conflicts in the Middle East. Since the 1990s, Greece received approximately one million migrants: co-ethnic returnees from the Soviet Union, Greek Albanians from South Albania, and economic migrants from Eastern European, Asian, and African countries.

In this context of economic strain, migrants, asylum seekers, and refugees have provided ready scapegoats. The extremist **Golden Dawn** party, with a platform aiming to rid Greece of 'illegal immigrants' was elected to the Greek Parliament for the first time in 2012. In July of 2012, Golden Dawn courted publicity by launching a Greeks-only blood drive: putting up posters in Athens calling for blood donations for a blood bank for native-born Greeks only.

The following month in August 2012, in front of the Greek Parliament building, Golden Dawn party members organized a Greeks-only free food handout to those with identity cards proving their Greek nationality. Excluded from such handouts were the large numbers of third-country nationals in Greece, many of whom are asylum seekers and irregular migrants living in deprived conditions in Athens. Inside the Greek Parliament in October 2012, one Golden Dawn Member of Parliament (MP) described migrants as "sub-human who have invaded our country, with all kinds of diseases" (Council of Europe 2013: 8). In 2014, Golden Dawn made further gains by securing 10 percent of the Greek vote in the European Parliament elections—gaining three seats. In the absence of official data, NGOs have noted that Greece has experienced a sharp rise in racist hostility and a consequent increase in racist hate crime.

In Hungary, as in Greece, a deepening economic crisis in the context of the global financial crisis, with rising unemployment, has provided fertile ground for nationalism, scapegoating, vilification, and attacks against minority communities. Hungary's Roma community has been a particular target. Anti-Roma rhetoric and the term 'Gypsy criminality' have been used by the right-wing nationalist Jobbik party and the Hungarian National Guard paramilitary organization in campaigning for national and European parliamentary elections. In 2010, Jobbik won seats in the Hungarian parliament for the first time after securing almost 17 percent of the vote. In 2014, Jobbik won three seats in the European Parliament after securing nearly 15 percent in the Hungarian vote for the European Parliament elections.

From the evidence of racist attacks against Roma/Gypsies/Travellers in Europe, a number of patterns can be observed (Iganski 2011). In common with other communities victimized by racist attacks, Roma experience harassment and assaults on an everyday basis while the offenders and those who are being targeted go about their everyday lives. However, Roma communities also appear to be more likely the object of mass violence perpetrated by mobs, crowds, and gangs of attackers, compared with other communities victimized in racist attacks.

Destruction and damage of property feature prominently in the occurrence of mass violence against Roma, betraying perhaps a particular virulence of anti-Roma sentiment. In some instances, the outcome of such attacks, likely to be intended by many perpetrators, is the expulsion and subsequent exclusion of Roma/Gypsies from the localities in which they live, amounting to an 'ethnic cleansing' of the areas involved.

Hate crime data for European countries beyond the European Union are severely limited. Through its Office for Democratic Institutions and Human Rights (ODIHR), the Organization for Security and Cooperation in Europe (OSCE) has published an annual report since 2008 documenting hate crime and policy responses across the OSCE region. The report makes publicly available data primarily drawn from hate crimes recorded by law enforcement agencies and supplemented by information provided by NGOs. However, no official hate crime data have been provided by almost a third of the OSCE countries (ODIHR 2013).

In the case though of one such country, Russia, the European Commission against Racism and Intolerance (ECRI) noted in its 2013 ECRI Report on the Russian Federation concern about a "high incidence" of racist violence targeted mainly against non-Slavs, migrants from the North Caucasus and Central Asian Countries, and migrants and visitors of African origin (ECRI 2013). About 20 percent of the population of the Russian Federation are from minority national and ethnic communities. Political struggles in the North Caucasus have stoked hostility and conflict against North Caucasians migrating within the Russian Federation. Migrants from other minority communities similarly face hostility which is reinforced by nationalist rhetoric in political and public discourse.

Widespread xenophobic sentiment in Russia provides the context for racist violence. In surveys of the Russian population conducted by the Moscow-based Levada Center in 2013, almost three-quarters (73 percent) of respondents agreed that migrants from the former Soviet Republics should be deported, just over half of the respondents (54 percent) agreed that immigration from the Caucasus should be restricted, and more than two out of five respondents (45 percent) agreed that restrictions should also apply to immigration from China and Central Asia (Russian Analytical Digest 2013: 8–9).

As in other European countries, social media provide a ready platform for racist and xenophobic sentiment in Russia. Social media outlets, such as Facebook, Instagram, and Vkontakte (VK.com, a Russian website similar to Facebook), are often used to propagate hate. One group which became well known for using social media for such purposes was Occupy Pedophilia. While Occupy Pedophilia mainly targeted sexual minorities, there were also instances where minority ethnic communities were subject to online hate. A 2014 article in *Americablog* contained screenshots of pictures from an Occupy Pedophilia member's Instagram account. In one picture, he held a swastika pendant up to the cameras while standing next to a man dressed in orthodox Jewish clothing. In another, a man is seen giving the middle finger to two black women with the captions "monkey," "n*gger," and "Metro zoo."

Antisemitism and Violence against Jews

In November 2013, the European Union Fundamental Rights Agency (FRA) published the results of its online survey of Jewish people's experiences of hate crime, discrimination, and antisemitism, carried out between September and October 2012 (FRA 2013a). Thirty percent of Hungarian Jewish respondents, the highest proportion out of all the countries in the survey, reported that they had personally experienced verbal insults, harassment, or physical attack on account of being Jewish in the last year. Forty-eight percent of the participants in Hungary—again the highest proportion out of all countries in the survey—reported that they had considered emigrating because they don't feel safe living in that country (see Figure 2.2). The Hungarian Ministry of Foreign Affairs responded by issuing a statement pointing to "flaws" in the survey methodology. However, in May 2013, the Prime Minister underlined Hungary's commitment to tackling amtisemitism in a speech to a meeting of the World Jewish Congress held in Budapest to draw attention to the problem in Hungary.

Violence against Jews is nested in widespread denigration and bigotry. Just before the 2014 conflict was being waged between Israel and Hamas, the Anti-Defamation League (ADL 2014) reported the results of a worldwide survey of attitudes toward Jews. By means of telephone and personal interviews, a representative sample of 53,100 people from 102 countries and territories covering 89 percent of the world's population was asked whether the following eleven different negative stereotypes about Jews were "probably true" or "probably false":

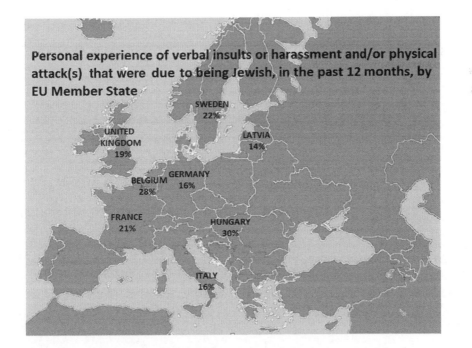

Figure 2.2 Hate crimes against Jews in Europe.
Source: FRA (2013).

- Jews are more loyal to Israel than to [this country/the countries they live in].
- Jews have too much power in the business world.
- Jews have too much power in international financial markets.
- Jews don't care about what happens to anyone but their own kind.
- Jews have too much control over global affairs.
- People hate Jews because of the way Jews behave.
- Jews think they are better than other people.
- Jews have too much control over the United States government.
- Jews have too much control over the global media.
- Jews still talk too much about what happened to them in the Holocaust.
- Jews are responsible for most of the world's wars.

As a measure of the pervasiveness of antisemitism, the ADL survey found that 26 percent of all respondents, worldwide, said that at least 6 of the 11, or a majority, of the negative stereotypes about Jews were "probably true." The degree of antisemitism was highest in Middle-Eastern and Northern-African countries (74 percent) and lowest among the Americas (19 percent) as well as Oceania countries including Australia, New Zealand, and Guam (14 percent).

The Spatial Impact of Racial, Ethnic, and Xenophobic Violence

As noted in Chapter 1, hate violence can have a profound impact upon people's behavior and, at the most extreme, it can lead to people fleeing the areas of victimization *en masse*. We noted such flight in Iraq, Myanmar, and India.

To date, the behavioral and spatial consequences of hate violence in relatively peaceful societies have not received the attention they deserve but have been marginalized in the scholarly hate crime literature. However, from the small amount of research that has been undertaken, using data from the Crime Survey for England and Wales concerning defensive and avoidance measures reportedly taken by small numbers of crime victims following victimization, there are indicators of different patterns between victims of hate crime and victims of otherwise motivated offenses. In the case of victims of household crime, it was evident that hate crime victims were more likely to report relocating their home and being more alert and less trusting of other people, while victims of otherwise motivated household crime were more likely to report increasing the security of their vehicles and valuables. In the case of victims of personal offenses, hate crime victims were more likely than victims of otherwise motivated crime to say that they had started to avoid walking in certain places (Iganski & Lagou 2014). However, much more research is needed to explore the particular behavioral impacts of hate violence beyond these limited survey findings.

A small number of qualitative studies provide some further insights into the spatial impact of hate crime victimization even in relatively peaceful societies. Participants in a study in Latvia published by the Latvian Center for Human Rights (Dzelme 2008) described how their spatial mobility, or their movement around town, was constrained as they sought to escape potential further victimization by avoiding seemingly risky places. Given that many attacks occur in public places—on the streets in residential neighborhoods as well as downtown, in shopping malls, on public transportation, and in places of leisure and recreation such as bars, sport arenas, cinema complexes—the confinement can be profoundly limiting.

The spatial impact of hate crime not only affects those who are direct victims. Others who share the same identity as the victim and who come to hear about the violence—perhaps family, friends, or other people in the neighborhood—can suffer the same intimidating impact and likewise take avoidance measures. Members of targeted communities carry mental maps of 'no go areas' in their heads (Rai & Hesse 1992: 177). They will understand that hate crimes are not personal: victims are attacked not for the persons they are, but for what their visible identity represents to the attacker. They realize that they could be next.

In extreme cases, members of a victimized group become fearful enough to contemplate making a permanent exodus from their homeland. Following a recent rash of antisemitic incidents—insults, physical violence, and discrimination—some 29 percent of European Jews considered emigrating because they no longer felt safe in their own countries (FRA 2013a, p. 37). In France, a large number followed through after a gunman in Toulouse murdered seven people at a Jewish school. In 2013, more than 3,000 French Jews immigrated to Israel. In the years 2014–15 that number was expected to reach 5,000 to 6,000, as a result of a terrorist attack on a Jewish grocery store in Paris which left four dead.

Understanding the Determinants of Racial, Ethnic, and Xenophobic Violence

Much of the focus by civil society organizations monitoring racist and xenophobic violence, and supporting and advocating for victims, is on extreme-right, neo-Nazi perpetrators. The same is the case for news media reporting of hate crime. Extremist attacks stand out. They are newsworthy, perhaps because they provide a contemporary glimpse into the dark history of modern Europe. However, attacks by extremists do not occur in a vacuum. The attitudes and the sentiments they convey in hate crimes are shared and underpinned by widespread denigration of the communities that are commonly the targets for their actions: people from minority ethnic, religious, and national communities; asylum seekers; migrants; and long-settled minority populations. They are constructed as the 'Other' and denigrated with respect to some difference of social significance.

While extremist offenders are the dramatic newsworthy end of the spectrum of hate crime offenders, far more numerous are the 'everyday' perpetrators involved in offending in the context of their ordinary lives. Such people don't sport Nazi insignia, don't attend far-right marches, don't consort with hard-line active extremists, and don't get involved in pre-planned or targeted violence. However, the ordinary offenders share many of the sentiments of the extremists, live in the same cultures of bigotry, and on occasion may even parrot extremist rhetoric when venting racist abuse.

Racial, ethnic, and xenophobic violence is spawned in cultures of endemic attitudes and values about particular people which socially construct them as different or the 'Other' in some extremely negative manner—as sub-humans, "mud people," or children of the devil. Hate-crime victims are very often chosen based on their racial, religious, or ethnic identity. In such incidents, the perpetrators may hold an ethnocentric attitude, believing that certain racial or religious affiliations are vastly inferior to their own. Stereotyped impressions come forth in support of the ethnocentric image—members of another group are treated as lazy, dirty, mercenary, violent, stupid, sly, deceitful, controlling, or sexually immoral.

This process appears to be universal across nation states although the particular communities subject to denigration vary depending upon the national context. Such denigration licenses discrimination, oppression, and violence.

Given the social context for racial, ethnic, and xenophobic violence, the responsibility for the violence extends beyond the direct perpetrator to the communities where the cultural values in which the violence is nested are pervasive. Such communities have therefore very aptly been called 'perpetrator communities' (Sibbitt 1997: 101) as the cultural context legitimizes and normalizes discriminatory violence. This is not only pertinent to understanding racial, ethnic, and xenophobic violence. In the next two chapters of this book, we discuss how homophobic and transphobic hate crimes, and hate crimes against people with disabilities, are also nested in cultural contexts of victim denigration.

QUESTIONS FOR DISCUSSION

1. Why do you think it is that many victims of racist crimes do not report them to the police?
2. What do you understand about scapegoating as a process behind racist violence?
3. What are the spatial impacts of racist violence, and how might they be accounted for?

3: Homophobic and Transphobic Violence

The stigmatization of people who do not conform to heterosexual gender norms is universal: it is pervasive across all nations around the globe. In many nations, antipathy against homosexuality is manifest in explicit inequalities in civil and criminal provisions. While there is a growing liberalization of attitudes toward homosexuality in many nations, persistent cultural and institutionalized animus provides a foundation for violence against lesbian, gay, bisexual, transgender and **queer** (LGBTQ) people. In this chapter, we discuss the scale of the problem and the cultural contexts in which homophobic and transphobic violence is nested.

The Scale of Homophobic and Transphobic Violence

One of the most comprehensive surveys to date of the experience of discrimination, harassment and violence against lesbian, gay, bisexual, transgender, and queer people was carried out by the European Union Fundamental Rights Agency (FRA) in 2012 (FRA 2013b). It revealed a disturbing picture of victimization.

In total, 93,079 persons aged 18 or older across the 27 EU Member States and Croatia, and identifying as lesbian, gay, bisexual, or transgender, provided information about their experiences through an online questionnaire. While the purposive nature of the sample means that the results cannot be generalized, the survey did capture the collective experiences of a very large number of people.

Six percent of all respondents said that they had been attacked or threatened with violence at least once in the past twelve months, partly or completely because they were perceived to be lesbian, gay, bisexual, or transgender. Most of the violence occurred in public places and was perpetrated often by more than one person and mostly males (FRA 2013b: 23). Transgender respondents reported the highest level of victimization—slightly above the average at 8 percent—and almost one in three victims had been attacked or threatened more than three times in the preceding 12 months (FRA 2013b: 21–23).

While the level of physical violence and threats was severe, even more prevalent was the experience of harassment. Almost a fifth (19 percent) of all respondents said that they had been victims of harassment in the past year partly or completely because they were perceived to be lesbian, gay, bisexual, or transgender. Lesbian women were the most likely to have been harassed—almost a quarter (23 percent) in the last year—along with transgender respondents, of whom 22 percent had been harassed in the preceding 12 months. A report of an online survey a few years earlier which recruited 2,669 solely transgender respondents from across the European Union suggested that the frequency of transphobic harassment experienced by transgender people, defined in the survey as including comments, verbal abuse, threatening behavior, and physical assault, may be greater than homophobic harassment experienced by lesbian women and gay men (Turner et al. 2009: 1). When harassment is defined broadly in this way it appears that the findings from the EU Fundamental Rights Agency survey do indicate a higher level of victimization for transgender people.

While the EU FRA survey captured non-fatal hate violence, the **National Coalition of Anti-Violence Programs** (NCAVP) in the United States has provided details of the annual numbers of homicides in the US involving lesbian, gay, bisexual, transgender, queer, and HIV-affected people (NCAVP 2013).

In 2012, 25 homicides were noted by the NCAVP to be hate-motivated—a decrease on the year before—but the fourth highest ever recorded by the NCAVP. The characteristics of the victims continued to reveal a trend that had been evident in previous years (NCAVP 2013: 21) in that the risk of homicide was greater for LGBTQ and HIV-affected people of color, transgender people of color, and transgender women, than other LGBTQ and HIV-affected people (see Figure 3.1).

Almost three-quarters of the homicide victims in 2012 were people of color, more than half were black and African American, and a little more than one in ten were white. Slightly more than three in ten of the victims were women—some identifying as transgender women. Overall, just over half of all victims were transgender. Disturbingly, given that the information was provided by NCAVP-member programs active in only 18 States in the US, the number of homicides recorded by the NCAVP will be an undercount.

Elsewhere in the Americas, the **United Nations High Commissioner for Human Rights** noted the murder of at least 31 LGBTQ persons over an 18-month period in Honduras (UNHCHR 2011: 9). In the case of Europe, the 2012 annual hate crimes report of the OSCE Office for Democratic Institutions and Human Rights (ODIHR 2013: 79–86) noted reports from NGOs and civil society organizations of bias-motivated murders of LGBTQ people in 2012 in Belgium, Germany, Hungary, Russia, and Turkey.

Understanding the Cultural Context of Homophobic and Transphobic Violence

We concluded the last chapter by discussing the cultural foundations of racial, ethnic, and xenophobic violence. Hate crimes which occur because of the victim's sexual

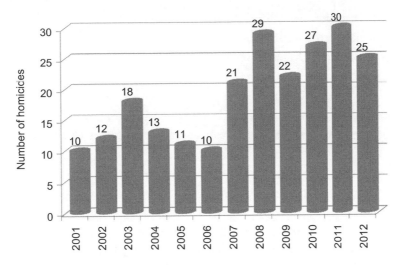

Figure 3.1 LGBTQ and HIV-affected victims of homicide in the United States 2001–2012.

Source: Adapted from National Coalition of Anti-Violence Programs (2013), page 21.

identity have been influentially conceptualized as a "logical, albeit extreme, extension" of cultures of heterosexism (Herek 1990: 316). Gregory Herek defined heterosexism as:

> an ideological system that denies, denigrates, and stigmatizes any non-heterosexual form of behavior, identity, relationship, or community. Like racism, sexism, and other ideologies of oppression, heterosexism is manifested both in societal customs and institutions, such as religion and the legal system (referred to here as cultural heterosexism), and in individual attitudes and behaviors (referred to here as psychological heterosexism).
>
> (Herek 1992: 89)

The prevalence of what Herek referred to as 'psychological heterosexism' was demonstrated by the Pew Research Center's 2013 Global Attitudes Survey in which 40,117 respondents from across 40 countries were interviewed about what are often considered to be moral concerns: extramarital affairs, gambling, homosexuality, abortion, premarital sex, alcohol consumption, divorce, and the use of contraceptives. Across the 40 countries surveyed, homosexuality was ranked the third in terms of unacceptability, although there was considerable variation across geographic regions (Pew Research Center 2014).

Respondents from Middle Eastern countries surveyed—Egypt, Jordan, the Palestinian Territories, Tunisia, Lebanon, and Turkey—were as a group the most likely to believe that homosexuality is unacceptable, although there is some variation in attitudes between these countries.

Large majorities of respondents from sub-Saharan African countries included in the survey also believed that homosexuality is unacceptable, although there was some divergence ranging from 98 percent of respondents in Ghana to 62 percent of respondents in South Africa.

In general, fewer respondents in the Latin American countries surveyed—El Salvador, Bolivia, Venezuela, Mexico, Brazil, Chile, and Argentina—believed that homosexuality is unacceptable compared with the Asian/Pacific countries covered in the survey. Yet there was considerable variation within these regions. In the Asian/Pacific region, 78 percent of respondents in Australia considered homosexuality as either acceptable or not a moral issue. By contrast, 93 percent of respondents in Indonesia believed that it is unacceptable.

Respondents from European countries were the most accepting of homosexuality, although in this region too there was considerable variation. In Spain, the vast majority, 93 percent, of respondents considered homosexuality as either acceptable or not a moral issue, whereas almost three-quarters of respondents in Russia believed it is unacceptable.

Overall, the Pew Research Center research has found a greater acceptance of homosexuality in more secular and affluent countries compared with poorer countries and nations with higher levels of religiosity. In general, younger respondents and women respondents were more accepting of homosexuality (Pew Research Center 2013).

In most nations, cultural heterosexism is manifest and reinforced in explicitly discriminatory civil and criminal provisions. In Europe in 2014, same-sex marriage was only legal in 12 countries: Belgium, England, France, Iceland, Luxembourg, the Netherlands, Norway, Portugal, Scotland, Spain, Sweden, and Wales. Most of these countries have only legalized same-sex marriage within the last five years. South Africa is the only African country in which same-sex marriage is legalized. Argentina, Brazil, Mexico (in some jurisdictions), and Uruguay are the only countries where it is legalized in South America. Nowhere else in the world, apart from more than 30 states and Washington DC in the United States, Canada, and New Zealand, was same-sex marriage lawful in 2014.

In respect of the criminal law, in 2014, homosexual acts were illegal in 78 countries, spanning some nations in Africa, Asia, the Middle East, Latin America and the Caribbean, and Oceania (Itaborahy & Zhuriminali 2014). In Latin America and the Caribbean, homosexual acts are primarily outlawed among the Caribbean nations: Antigua and Barbuda, Barbados, Belize, Dominica, Grenada, Guyana, Jamaica, St. Kitts and Nevis, St. Lucia, St. Vincent and the Grenadines, and Trinidad and Tobago.

Homosexual acts are legal in all countries of Europe and in North America. However, in a retrogressive step, laws prohibiting the promotion of homosexuality were introduced in Belarus, Latvia, the Russian Federation, and Ukraine in 2013 and in Lithuania in 2014 (Itaborahy & Zhuriminali 2014: 66).

In the African country of Mauritania, in 2014 same-sex sexual activities between men were punishable by public stoning to death (while women are sentenced to imprisonment and fine). The death penalty for men also applied in some northern states in Nigeria where the maximum penalty for sexual acts between women was whipping and/or imprisonment. The death penalty is also imposed by the Islamist extremist group **Al Shabab** in southern parts of Somalia. In March 2013, after a conviction for sodomy, a gay Somali teen was reportedly stoned to death in front of villagers (Bennett-Smith 2013).

In the Middle East in 2014, the death penalty was also in force in Iran for sodomy (defined under the Islamic Penal Code of Iran as sexual intercourse between men [Itaborahy & Zhuriminali 2014: 57]), Saudi Arabia, where the penalty for a married man committing such homosexual acts is death by stoning, and for an unmarried man is 100 strikes of the whip along with banishment for a year (Itaborahy & Zhuriminali 2014: 62). The same penalties and differential treatment between married and unmarried men also apply in Yemen. Consensual sex between women in Yemen is punishable by up to three years of imprisonment (Itaborahy & Zhuriminali 2014: 66).

Overall, it can be seen that heterosexism, or 'heteronormativity'—the notion that heterosexuality, sexual and marital relations between women and men, and sex-specific gender roles are the norm (Action Aid 2009: 6)—is woven into the social, cultural, and legal fabric of many nations and consequently provides an enabling environment for anti-queer violence. Such violence might be regarded as an act of punishment and, in some instances, acts of correction for those who transgress the boundaries of heteronormativity. So-called 'corrective rape' of lesbian women, in which violence on the basis of sexual orientation and gender intersect, provides a case in point. The notion of 'corrective rape' refers to the rape of lesbian women committed by men to punish the women for their sexual orientation and to 'cure' them of their lesbianism (Action Aid 2009: 5). Some of the verbal abuse reported by survivors of 'corrective rape' in South Africa attest to perpetrators' motives: they were told they were "being taught a lesson," "being shown how to be a real woman," meant to experience "what a real man tasted like" (Action Aid 2009:12). Even school children have featured among the perpetrators and the victims of 'corrective rape,' according to the **South African Human Rights Commission** (South African Human Rights Commission 2008: 9). Black lesbians are reportedly more at risk because of their disadvantaged position relative to white women. (Action Aid 2009: 8).

However, to understand why *particular* acts of homophobic and transphobic violence occur, as is the case with other types of hate violence, we need to look at the offender's state of mind and the interactional dynamics of the circumstances which precipitate the offense, as ultimately hate violence is a micro-level phenomenon—an interaction between individuals. We address this, in the case of all types of hate violence, when examining the motivations and impulses for hate crime offending in Chapters 7 and 8 of this book.

QUESTIONS FOR DISCUSSION

1. Do you think there is a relationship between cultural and psychological heterosexism?
2. In what ways might cultural heterosexism provide a foundation for homophobic and transphobic violence?
3. How might homophobic and transphobic violence serve as punishment for transgression of heteronormativity?

4:   Disablist Violence

T he United Nations has proposed that persons with disabilities—
defined as people with long-term physical, mental, intellectual, or sensory
impairments—constitute the world's "largest and most disadvantaged minority" (UN 2007: 1). In 2007, the UN estimated that 650 million people around the
world live with a disability. That number is growing as the world's population increases,
people are living longer, and health technology constantly evolves. People with disabilities, however, are over-represented among those living in poverty and, universally,
they face discrimination and marginalization. According to the UN, "In most parts
of the world, there are deep and persistent negative stereotypes and prejudices against
persons with certain conditions and differences" (UN 2007: 3).

There is a dearth of global data, however, on violence against people with disabilities. While people with a physical or mental disability of some form in many nations,
cultures, and communities have long suffered denigration, hostility, and even violence
because of their disability, it is only in recent years that the notion of disability or
'**disablist**' violence and disability hate crime has begun to be articulated in a small
number of countries and primarily through social movement activism.

The 2012, annual hate crimes report published by the OSCE's Office for Democratic Institutions and Human Rights noted that only 14 of the 57 OSCE participating states covering Europe, Central Asia, and North America reported collecting any
official data on disability-motivated hate crime. Figures were provided to ODIHR by
only four countries (ODIHR 2013: 89). Among them, the United Kingdom stands
out as an exception in terms of the recognition of the problem of disablist violence
and the official monitoring of disability hate crime—mostly because of vigorous campaigning by disability rights activists.

According to estimates from the Crime Survey for England and Wales for 2011–12
and 2012–13, there were 62,000 incidents of disability-motivated crime per year on
average (UK Home Office, ONS, MoJ 2013: 26). One-third of these offenses involved
physical violence against the person with six out of ten resulting in injury, and nearly
a third (30 percent) involved public-order offenses such as harassment or verbal abuse
causing alarm or distress.

The reality of the violence experienced by people with disabilities stokes a greater
fear of violence compared with people without disabilities. Analysis of the Crime

Survey for England and Wales has shown that disabled women and men are more likely than non-disabled women and men to be worried about being a victim of crime. They are more likely to feel unsafe when walking alone after dark, more likely than non-disabled women and men to be worried about being physically attacked by strangers, and more likely to worry about being insulted or pestered by someone. On each of these measures, disabled women express greater levels of worry about victimization than disabled men (Nocon et al. 2011).

In the United States in 2012, 11 percent of the victims of the 293,790 hate crimes estimated for that year by the National Crime Victimization Survey believed that the offenders were motivated by bias against their disability (Wilson 2014: 3). However, only the most egregious cases make the news. In a suburban area outside of Pittsburgh, Pennsylvania, in February 2010, 31-year-old Jennifer Daugherty, a mentally disabled woman, was murdered by six people pretending to be her good friends. Getting her alone in a vulnerable position, the perpetrators tortured Daugherty for days by shaving her head; binding her with Christmas decorations; beating her with a towel rack and vacuum cleaner; feeding her detergent, urine, and various medications; and then stabbing her to death (Levin 2013; Martinez 2010).

This attack on a person with a mental disability was anything but unique, yet few Americans are aware of the special susceptibility of people with disabilities to extraordinary violence. Thinking of crimes inspired by hate or bias, they may conjure up an image of a burning cross on the lawn of a black family, or swastikas scrawled on the walls of a synagogue, but they are unlikely to think of the brutal murder of Jennifer Daugherty. Or the five staff members working in a Louisiana psychiatric facility who, in 2008, battered their patients with hand weights and inserted bleach into their open wounds (Levin 2013). Or the 19-year-old Boston man with a developmental disability who was thrown to the ground by a group of nine young people who repeatedly kicked, beat, and choked him in 2010 (McFarqhuar 1999). Readers are welcome to visit the Brudnick Center website at Northeastern University (http://www.northeastern.edu/brudnickcenter/), where you will find a link to a 15-minute documentary film about disablist violence titled Three Times the Violence.

Not unlike racism, antisemitism, and homophobia, the negative perceptions of disability are formed very early in a child's life. The majority of children ages three to six are already aware of physical disabilities and have already attributed negative characteristics to those who are not physically able bodied; they are more likely to learn about psychiatric and intellectual deficits a few years later, when their cognitive abilities have developed enough to think of people who are developmentally different in unflattering terms. Later in life, what began as an aversion may easily be transformed into outright prejudice and hate.

Derogatory language about people with disabilities is well-known and perpetuates stereotypes. Research carried out by the National Association for Mental Health

(Mind 2007) in England with a sample of 304 people with severe or long-term mental health problems living in the community provided numerous examples of disparaging language. Sixty-two percent of the research participants said that they had been verbally harassed with taunting about their mental distress in the past two years. Insults hurled included: "'psycho,' 'loony,' 'schizo,' 'nutter,' 'freak,' 'mad,' 'not all there,' 'round the bend,' 'thick,' 'stupid,' 'no brains,' 'wrong in the head,' 'obsessive'" (Mind 2007: 6).

Yet violence against people with disabilities differs in important ways from other hate crimes. Unlike racially motivated offenses, disablist attacks tend to be committed less by strangers and more by family members, neighbors, and friends who may also be caregivers (Wolfe 1995). Victims are reluctant to report attacks out of fear that their tormentors will retaliate. Or, they may have a psychiatric or intellectual difficulty which interferes with their capacity to recognize false friendships or to report a crime. In the United Kingdom, the term 'mate crime' (Thomas 2011) has been coined to refer to such offenses.

Hate violence can occur at the intersections that bring together identity characteristics. Disabled women are a particular case in point whereby gender and disability combined raise the risk of violence significantly. While they are subject to the same types of violence experienced separately by women—physical and sexual violence, emotional and verbal abuse—women and girls who possess disabilities are seen to be at greater risk as they are particularly targeted by some perpetrators who regard them as especially vulnerable. The **World Health Organization** (WHO) has noted that people with disabilities are more at risk of violence and sexual abuse than people without disabilities (WHO 2011: 59). Studies in Canada (Cohen et al. 2005), the United States (Smith 2008), and Taiwan (Lin et al. 2009) have found that disabled women are more likely to experience sexual violence than non-disabled women. According to Justice Department statistics, Americans with disabilities are almost four times more likely than Americans in the general population in the same age categories to be victims of sexual assaults (Harrell 2014). In 2012, Human Rights Watch drew attention to the forced sterilization of women and girls with disabilities occurring across the globe, pointing out that such acts are not only acts of violence, but also acts of social control and the denial of fundamental human rights (Human Rights Watch 2011).

As we shall discuss in Chapter 7, only a very small minority of hate crimes directly involve organized hate groups. Disability hate crimes are no different in this respect. However, it is important to acknowledge that some organized hate groups overtly display their hostility to disabled people. In early November 2002, for example, the Internet discussion forum of the white supremacist group Stormfront allocated a section of its forum to eugenics. Among the disablist comments presented online was the following: "We must put into place social and economic systems that encourage the best genes to dominate in numbers as well as power."

The Cultural Basis of Disablist Violence

We have proposed in the preceding chapters, in applying a global perspective to the problem of hate violence, that hate and prejudice are typically aspects of the normal state of affairs of the society in which they exist. It might be more comfortable if we were able to characterize hate and prejudice as deviant, irrational, and pathological behavior—as existing in the domain of a few 'extremists' on the margins of society. At the extreme, it is true that a relatively small number of cases of hate crimes have been inspired by the delusional thinking of the perpetrator. Yet, the existence of hate hardly depends on individual pathology or abnormal psychology. Nor is it a form of deviance from the point of view of mainstream society. Even if the admission of being prejudiced is unacceptable, hate itself is instead normal, rational, and conventional. It is part of the culture—the way of life—of the society in which it exists, appealing typically to the most conventional and traditional of its members (Westie 1964; Feagin & Vera 1995; Barnett 1999).

Where it is cultural, sympathy for a particular hatred may become a widely shared and enduring element in the normal state of affairs of a group of people. Even more important, the prejudice may become systematically organized to reward individuals who are bigoted and cruel and to punish those individuals who are caring and respectful of differences (Katz 1993). In such circumstances, tolerance for group differences may actually be regarded as rebellious behavior and those who openly express tolerance may be viewed as rebels.

In the case of disablist hate crime, an edifice of stereotypes, prejudices, and bigotry about people with disabilities provides a ready climate for violence. The stigmatization of people with disabilities is universal across nations as testified by a considerable body of research evidence, although the degree and nature of stigmatization differs with different disabilities as well as social environments. A study of stigma toward schizophrenia in the general population in Brazil showed a high level of adherence to negative stereotypes (Loch et al. 2014). A study in South Africa found that schizophrenia, and also substance abuse, were stigmatized significantly more than other mental health disorders (Sorsdahl & Stein 2010). Even with growing knowledge and understanding among the general population about the biological foundation of much mental ill-health (what is known as greater 'mental health literacy'), attitudes towards mental illness do not seem to have changed in the 21st century (Schomerus et al. 2012).

Just as in the last chapter we noted that homophobic and transphobic violence can only be understood in the context of cultural heternormativity, violence against disabled people can only be comprehended in the context of the background cultures of disablism and ableism. Characteristic of disabling culture is the pathologization and individualization of physical, mental, and intellectual impairment, notions of normality and abnormality (Goodley & Runswick-Cole 2011), and a discourse of 'ableism' whereby ability is revered and characterized as "fully human" and disability disparaged as a lesser state of human being (Campbell 2008: 153). From this perspective, impairment is seen as "inherently negative which should, if the opportunity presents itself, be ameliorated, cured or indeed eliminated" (Campbell 2008: 154). Thus, people with disabilities can be easily dehumanized. They can't walk or run, can't talk, can't think clearly, can't see or hear, or can't cope with everyday frustrations. In stereotyped portrayals, they lack the qualities associated with being a member of the human race.

However, while the background cultural edifice of attitudes about people with disabilities provides a necessary condition for hate crime to occur, as is the case with the other types of hate violence discussed in previous chapters, this does not explain everything. Some fundamental questions are left unanswered. Chiefly, if prejudice, bigotry, and bias are intricately woven into the socio-cultural fabric of many nations, which we and many others suggest that it is, then why is it that only certain people commit acts of hate violence when others in the same circumstances do not? To answer this question we need to look at the interaction between the offenders' states of mind, their character, their biography, and the circumstances in which they find themselves that precipitate the offense. Therefore, while hate violence is a global phenomenon, to fully understand it, we need to understand the interactional dynamics in which particular acts of hate crime are nested. This is the challenge that we undertake when we consider the motivations of hate crime offenders in Chapters 7 and 8. Before that, in the next chapter, we complete our whirlwind review of the problem of hate violence by considering the problem posed by violence against women.

QUESTIONS FOR DISCUSSION

1. In what ways is disablist violence similar to, but also different from, other types of hate violence?
2. How might the use of particular language serve to perpetuate disparaging stereotypes about people with disabilities?
3. Could disablist violence possibly be the most prevalent type of hate crime world-wide?

5: Violence against Women

When considering hate violence globally, a particular fact stands out: violence against women, most of it committed by intimate partners, is pervasive in all nations, cultures, and communities. While there is a vast amount of literature on the problem, the issue of violence against women has been on the margins of hate crime scholarship and subject to debate about whether it can be conceptualized as hate crime. The analytical approach that we take in this book, however, is to frame violence against women squarely as a form of hate crime—for reasons that we explain in this chapter.

Violence against Women: A Universal Problem

The scale of the problem of violence against women cannot be exaggerated. The World Health Organization concluded in 2013 that violence against women is "a global health problem of epidemic proportions requiring urgent action" (WHO 2013: 3). Presenting for the first time aggregated global and regional estimates of the prevalence of violence against women from systematic reviews of population data, the WHO estimated that more than a third (35.6 percent) of women around the world have at least one experience of physical or sexual intimate partner violence, sexual violence from a non-partner, or both (WHO 2013). The prevalence of intimate partner violence among women with a partner at the time of the survey or before was estimated to be 30 percent globally. The prevalence of non-partner sexual violence against women was estimated to be 7.2 percent globally.

The estimates also indicated an already high prevalence of intimate partner violence in young women's relationships. Globally, just over 29 percent of ever-partnered 15–19-year-olds experienced such violence. For all the estimates, only physical and sexual violence was included. The estimated prevalence of violence against women would be greater still if verbal and emotional violence were counted (see Figure 5.1).

Among the incidents of violence, the WHO estimated that 38 percent of all murders of women were perpetrated by male intimate partners—males with whom they had a romantic or intimate relationship. However, the consequences even of non-fatal violence against women can also be severe and long-lasting, as will be discussed in the next chapter of this book.

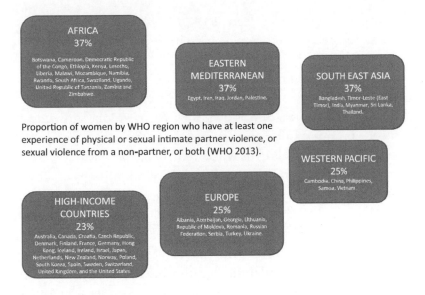

Figure 5.1 Intimate partner violence: A global problem.

In addition to violence by an intimate partner and sexual violence committed by someone other than a partner, other forms of violence against women include honor killings, female genital mutilation, the trafficking of women into prostitution, forced labor, and even forced marriage.

In regions of conflict, sexual violence against women and girls including rape, mutilation, sexual exploitation, and other abuse has been used as a deliberate weapon of war. **UNICEF**'s The State of the World's Children 1996 report noted that in the conflict in Bosnia and Herzegovina and Croatia in the early 1990s, more than 20,000 Muslim women and teenage girls had been raped. Rape was also systemically used in Rwanda as an act of ethnic cleansing (UNICEF 1996: 19). When rape is used as a weapon of war, women are forcibly impregnated to carry the enemy's child in an attempt to ethnically cleanse the next generation (Amnesty International 2004).

Studies of sexual violence used for '**ethnic cleansing**' in conflict zones indicate the severe long-lasting trauma inflicted on female victims. In a study of 65 women who were survivors of systematic mass rapes (Lončar et al. 2006), conducted during and shortly after the 1992–95 war in Croatia and Bosnia and Herzegovina, we learn that a third of the women were raped every day and by different rapists while held captive and most were physically and sexually tortured in further ways. In a number of cases, the rapists were victims' neighbors. The study illuminates the profound and enduring mental health impact inflicted. While none of the women had a history of psychiatric disorder before the rape, approximately a year after the violence had occurred, a majority suffered from depression, more than half manifested 'social phobias,' and almost a third reported suffering post-traumatic stress disorder. Seventeen out of twenty-nine women who became pregnant as a consequence of their rape had an induced abortion, with the decision to abort their pregnancies precipitated by suicidal thoughts and impulses. Among the twelve women who gave birth, only one kept the baby: the rest were given up for adoption.

Beyond conflict zones the news media generally only report the most brutal acts of sexual violence committed by strangers in public places. One such notorious attack in December 2012 was the subject of worldwide media attention, throwing the spotlight on sexual violence in India. In this brutal episode, a 23-year-old medical student was beaten and gang raped on a Delhi bus while on her way home after watching a film at a multiplex in an upscale shopping mall. She died of her injuries in a hospital almost two weeks later. The bus driver was among those arrested. He was later found dead in jail.

Notably, six months before the attack, India was ranked the worst country in which to be a woman among the G20 countries in a perceptions poll of 370 expert gender specialists—aid professionals, academics, health workers, policymakers, and development specialists. The survey was carried out by TrustLaw, a legal news service run by the Thomson Reuters Foundation; its findings were released ahead of the G20 heads of state summit meeting in Mexico in June 2012. Saudi Arabia, Indonesia, South Africa, and Mexico accompanied India in the bottom five rankings. In addition to sexual violence, female infanticide, child marriage, and slavery accounted for India's bottom spot (see Figure 5.2).

In September 2013, four men were found guilty and sentenced to death by a Delhi court for the December 2012 brutal gang rape of the 23-year-old medical student. The crime triggered a seemingly unprecedented wave of protest on the streets, particularly by young people—many of whom seemed to identify with the victim. The Indian government subsequently established a panel chaired by retired Justice Verma to recommend legal reform and other ways of tackling episodes of sexual violence. The panel's 644-page report for the Indian prime minister (Verma et al. 2013), produced in 30 days, made recommendations for reforms to policing and the training of criminal justice personnel, educational reforms, and the provision of rape-crisis centers. Legislative reforms also followed through the Criminal Law (Amendment) Act of 2013 passed by India's Parliament which came into force in February 2013.

Intimate Partner Violence

News media reporting of the most brutal acts of violence against women plays a valuable role in drawing attention to the problem. Such reporting, however, conveys a distorted picture. Far more prevalent and rather more routine are the everyday acts of violence, intimidation, and abuse committed by partners in intimate relationships—the type of violence shown by the World Health Organization to be the most prevalent.

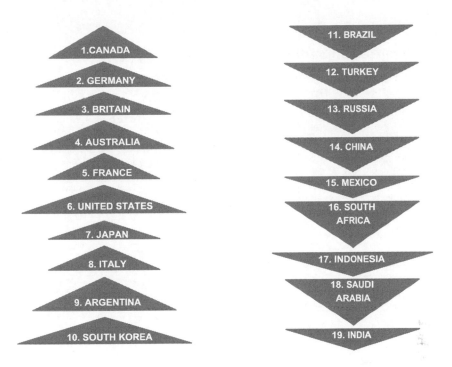

Figure 5.2 Best and worst ranked G20 countries to be a woman.

Source: Katharine Baldwin, 'Canada best G20 country to be a woman, India worst: TrustLawpoll', 13 June 2012. http://www.trust.org/item/?map=poll-canada-best-g20-country-to-be-a-woman-india-worst/

In the case of Europe, findings from the first ever survey of violence against women across the 28 **EU Member States** published in 2014 by the European Union Agency for Fundamental Rights (FRA) illuminated the extent of the problem. The survey covered 45,000 women aged between 18 and 74 years across the European Union who were selected by multi-stage random sampling and interviewed in their homes in person by female interviewers. It revealed that over one-third of women across the European Union have experienced physical and/or sexual violence since the age of 15 (see Figure 5.3).

The survey also assessed the short-term emotional responses and long-term psychological consequences of violent victimization. Overall, the reported impact of sexual violence was greater than the impact of physical violence, and the long-term psychological impact was greater when the perpetrator was a partner (FRA 2014: 56–58):

- Women who had experienced sexual violence were more likely to report feeling fearful, ashamed, embarrassed, and guilty. There was little difference between victims of partner and non-partner sexual violence in reporting these emotional reactions.
- Women victims of sexual violence by a partner were less likely to report feelings of shock—possibly because the violence was part of a continuum of abuse.

European Union Agency for Fundamental Rights (FRA) (2014)

☒ One in 3 women has experienced physical and/or sexual violence since the age of 15.

☒ An estimated 13 million women across the EU experienced physical violence and 3.7 million women experienced sexual violence in the course of the 12 months prior to the survey — together accounting for 8% of women across the EU.

☒ Just over a fifth (22%) of all women who had a current or previous partner at the time of the survey had experienced physical and/or sexual violence by a partner since the age of 15. The highest reported rates of such violence were in the Denmark (32%), Latvia (32%), Finland (30%), the United Kingdom (29%), and Sweden (28%). Austria, Croatia, Poland, Slovenia, and Spain each had the lowest reported rate of 13%.

☒ The most common forms of physical violence experienced by women involve pushing or shoving, slapping or grabbing, or the pulling of hair.

☒ Just over 1 in 10 women (11%) have experienced some form of sexual violence since they were 15 years old, either by a partner or some other person.

☒ One in 20 women (5%) has been raped since the age of 15.

☒ 43% of ever-partnered women have experienced some form of psychological violence in their relationships including both controlling and psychologically abusive behavior.

☒ Almost 1 in 5 (18%) women have experienced some form of stalking since the age of 15, and 5%, or an estimated 9 million women across the EU, experienced stalking in the 12 months prior to the survey.

☒ The prevalent forms of stalking are threatening, offensive or silent phone calls, followed by someone waiting or loitering where a women works or lives, then following around, or both. One in 20 (5%) women have been stalked by e-mail, text, or instant messaging since the age of 15.

Figure 5.3 Violence against women: An EU-wide survey.

- While the emotional reactions of women victims of physical violence were less pronounced than victims of sexual violence, victims of physical violence by a partner were more likely to report feelings of fear, shame, and embarrassment, than victims of non-partner violence.

- A majority of victims of physical and sexual violence by partners and non-partners reported long-term psychological consequences. For both physical and sexual violence, long-term psychological impacts were more likely to be reported by victims where the violence was perpetrated by a partner—possibly as a consequence of repeated victimization or the ongoing fear of further violence.

- The long-term psychological impact of sexual violence was also more pronounced than the impact of physical violence. Victims of sexual violence by partners and non-partners were more likely to report long-term psychological impacts and more likely to report experiencing a combination of impacts.

Conceptualizing Violence against Women as 'Hate Crime'

A fundamental argument made against conceptualizing violence against women as hate violence and hate crime is that the perpetrators don't 'hate' all women in the way that a person who commits a religiously aggravated or racist attack, for instance, 'hates' all people of the group they have targeted (Weisburd & Levin 1994: 35). Furthermore, violence against women also stands out in that, as discussed in this chapter, the violence is more likely to be committed by someone with whom a woman has a relationship rather than a stranger who targets them in a random attack. The violent stranger fits the common conception of the hate crime perpetrator, but not the overall reality of female victimization.

These arguments, however, hinge on a misnomer afflicting the very concept of 'hate violence' and 'hate crime.' The term 'hate crime' provides an emotive banner under which to rally opposition to discriminatory violence. But the sentiment of 'hate' is only rarely present in the impulses driving so-called 'hate crime' offenders. Other sentiments and emotions are often at work, as we discuss in Chapters 7 and 8.

There is a common denominator to hate violence: the violence is rooted in the denigration of the victim's identity. As we noted in previous chapters, perpetrators' actions are not manifestations of pathological minds. They are entirely rational. The perpetrators are acting out cultural values which they have imbibed. Hate violence is an act of power: the perpetrators are asserting their superiority and place above the victim. Accordingly, in the case of intimate partner violence, scholars and policy makers have recognized that such violence is not simply a private matter between two persons (cf. Isaacs 2001). Instead, it is incubated in cultures of endemic patriarchal attitudes and values about women's place—a subordinate position relative to men—in social and personal relations.

The same values also underpin other forms of violence against women. Such cultural attitudes are pervasive and universal across nation states and communities although the precise dimensions and intensity differ according to particular local contexts. These values encourage and support, sometimes consciously and other times sub-consciously, oppressive social practices ranging from unequal respect to unequal opportunity to discriminatory treatment to emotional and verbal abuse to direct acts of physical violence, which subordinate, disadvantage, and damage women. Such practices are not only the visible expression of the underlying values which inform oppressive actions, but the practices themselves also sustain and reinforce the background cultural context by rendering it visible, by drawing attention to the prevalence of attitudes and values which underpin violence and other oppressive practices against women. There is therefore a symbiotic, mutually reinforcing, relationship between culture and action.

The social construction of heterosexual masculinity is integral to cultural attitudes about women's place in society, and it plays a fundamental role in male violence against women. It is appropriate to think of a number of constructions of different 'masculinities'—notions of what it means to be a man and how men are expected to behave—within an overarching notion of 'hegemonic masculinity' (Connell 1995). At the core of the construction of masculinity within many nations is the idea of the male as the 'breadwinner' engaged in the world of work to earn a living for their family. By corollary, women have been centrally constructed as dependent and subservient in the role of 'homemakers.' This notion isn't fixed—it is fluid and dynamic, and it has been changing over time. Nevertheless, strong remnants of the male breadwinner role persist to one degree or another in various nations.

Some elements of masculinity appear at first sight to be contradictory. Violence against women is deemed to be inappropriate and unmanly given the assumed imbalance in physical strength and fighting prowess between men and women. However, threats to masculinity can evoke anxiety, shame, and anger and provoke aggression—especially when the person's self-esteem is fragile, as we discuss in Chapter 8. For some men, when challenged by women, often in intimate partner relationships, when they feel slighted or humiliated, violence is a way of putting women back in line, back in their place, so as to reduce any challenge to the male advantage.

Given the social context for violence against women, responsibility also extends beyond the direct perpetrator to the communities where the cultural values nesting violence is pervasive. The direct perpetrators, however, are not simply automatons unthinkingly impelled by the particular values they have imbibed. There are also countervailing cultural values at work. For instance, despite its practice, the exercise of unrestrained violence is also universally condemned. The individual perpetrator of violence against women therefore exercises agency, makes an active choice between competing values even in emotionally charged situations, and is therefore responsible for their own actions. This dynamic relationship between social and individual context in the case of hate crime is a theme we return to when analyzing offender impulses in Chapters 7 and 8.

QUESTIONS FOR DISCUSSION

1. What are the arguments against conceptualizing violence against women as 'hate violence'?
2. In what ways does the prevailing culture in many nations serve to legitimize violence against women?
3. To what extent is violence against women a problem of masculinity?

6:   The Brutality of Hate

Why should hate violence be singled out for particular concern, as it is in this book? The reason is quite clear: There is something more egregious about hate-motivated violence than about other kinds of violent criminal behavior. In situations of mass conflict such as wars and civil wars, the impact of violence is rarely, if ever, confined to the armed combatants. Civilian populations too suffer profoundly as human collateral damage. In conflicts motivated around ethnic and religious hatred, or where such hatred plays a role in inter-communal conflicts, civilian populations are not collateral damage, they are the deliberate target of violence, indiscriminately victimized because of their identity. And while numerous types of violence can constitute crimes against humanity, hatred has featured prominently in such crimes as demonstrated in the genocidal slaughter of Tutsi and moderate Hutu ethnic groups in Rwanda in 1994, and the massacre of Bosnian Muslim men and boys by elements of the Bosnian Serb army during the 1992–1995 Bosnian war, and more recently in the 21st century in Iraq as discussed in Chapter 1 of this book. The targeting of women in sexual violence was also characteristic of these conflicts, used to intimidate, inflict terror, and ethnically cleanse.

Wars are often waged because of disputes involving land, markets, or other resources. Hatred may not be the primary cause of such conflicts. But it is an important aggravating factor that keeps warfare from being resolved.

Hate violence is a discriminatory form of violence, and even for relatively socially stable societies there is evidence, as we will discuss in this chapter, to show that discriminatory violence is more egregious than other forms of violence. Most victims of violence suffer some post-victimization impact. The victim might suffer physical injury, experience emotional and psychological consequences, and manifest behavioral changes. In the case of hate violence, however, the harms inflicted can potentially be greater than identical but otherwise motivated violence. As we will discuss in this chapter, a substantial body of evidence about the personal injuries of hate crime shows that, on average, hate crimes have the potential to hurt more than otherwise motivated crime. The impact of hate violence can also extend well beyond the person who is on the immediate receiving end, the person conventionally thought of as the 'victim.' Hate crime sends a message to everyone who shares the victim's identity: this could be you.

In analyzing in this chapter these key dimensions of the impact of hate globally, we will distinguish between the consequences of large-scale, mass hate violence and the routine everyday hate violence more characteristic of relatively stable and secure nations.

Fatal Hate Violence

In the 21st century, as before, there have been episodes of large-scale killings around the world in which denigration of the victims' identities and violent mobilization around ethnic and religious identity play a role, as discussed in Chapter 1 of this book. Hate violence also claims lives in relatively more socially stable parts of the world, such as the United States and Western Europe, as we will demonstrate, although the numbers of deaths may be far fewer and usually occur from isolated attacks rather than incidents of mass violence.

Official data on such fatalities are unreliable and do not reflect the actual number of cases. In the United States, the Federal Bureau of Investigation's (FBI) Uniform Crime Reports Hate Crime Data provide some limited evidence about the annual numbers of hate-motivated deaths, although as discussed in Chapter 2 the FBI data—based on voluntary police reports—provide an undercount of the true extent of the problem of hate crime.

According to FBI data, in the first decade of the 21st century, the number of lives claimed by hate-motivated murders and non-negligent manslaughter in the US ranged from 3 and 10 deaths annually. The vast majority of recorded hate crimes are non-fatal, involving either simple assault or aggravated assault (see Figure 6.1). Also, a substantial number of offenses involve threats or damage to property in the form of bias intimidation. These figures suggest a possible different pattern to the routine violence in countries characterized by relative social stability compared with countries experiencing episodes of outbreaks of mass violence which result in spikes in the number of fatalities.

However, it should be emphasized that a hate-motivated murder may not be recorded as a hate crime by the FBI because of lack of independent evidence that it was motivated by bias, even when victims and their families are convinced that they were singled out for abuse because of some difference. Even a brutal murder may not be classified as a hate crime, despite the fact that no other motive can be determined and bias seems obvious to objective observers. As a result, it is clear that the number of recorded hate-motivated murders is underestimated in FBI data.

In October 2006, for example, a mother of six, wearing a hijab (the head scarf of a devout Muslim woman) and carrying a three-month-old infant in her arms, was gunned down while walking on a residential street in Fremont, California, a relatively affluent and leafy city close to Silicon Valley. Because her assailant did not leave any

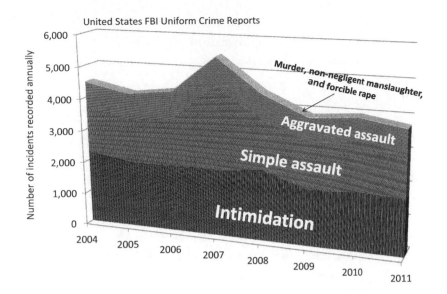

Figure 6.1 Bias incidents against persons.

indication of his intent at the crime scene—no slurs, no graffiti, no hate literature or tattoos, the motivation for this murder was not definitively identified. Yet relatives of the victim as well as local Muslim leaders who ruled out such other possibilities as robbery and revenge were convinced that this crime was motivated by hate (Kuruvila & Lee 2006). The killer had a lengthy criminal record, but no history of committing hate crimes. He and his victim were total strangers. The killer was convicted of murder, but hate motivation was not regarded as an aggravating factor.

Is Hate Violence "Excessively Brutal"?

In focusing on non-fatal violence, two decades ago, one of the foundational books for hate crime scholarship in the United States concluded that hate violence is generally more brutal than other forms of violence. In *Hate Crimes: The Rising Tide of Bigotry and Bloodshed*, Levin and McDevitt argued that there was a tendency for hate violence to be "excessively brutal" (Levin & McDevitt 1993: 11). Their conclusion left a significant footprint of understanding on the hate crime literature. Half of the 452 hate crimes recorded in the early 1990s by the Boston, Massachusetts, police that Levin and McDevitt analyzed involved assaults and other personal attacks—far exceeding the rate for otherwise motivated crimes. Hate crimes were also apparently more likely to result in physical injury to the victim, and hate crime victims were seemingly more likely to wind up in the hospital than victims of otherwise motivated crimes.

Since Levin and McDevitt's observations from Boston police records, analysis of the physical injuries inflicted by hate violence has not featured prominently in the expanding body of evidence on the impact of hate crime. Most studies have focused primarily on the emotional and psychological injuries inflicted that we will discuss in this chapter. However, a recent study revisited Levin and McDevitt's conclusion about the brutality of hate crimes by analyzing data from the Crime Survey for England and Wales (Iganski & Lagou 2014).

Crime survey data provide more reliable samples than police records to estimate whether hate crimes are especially violent relative to otherwise motivated crimes, given that it is well-known, as we noted in Chapter 2, that police-recorded crime provides only a partial picture of crime victimization. The analysis showed that just over half of all hate crimes reported in the survey were violent crimes (not too dissimilar to the FBI hate crime data), far exceeding—in fact, two-and-half times more than—the proportion of violent crimes to otherwise motivated crime. While these findings at first sight seem to indicate that hate crime is particularly more violent than otherwise motivated crime, they also indicate that the repertoire of offending by hate crime perpetrators is narrower than in otherwise motivated crimes: relatively fewer hate crime offenses involve auto-theft and house-breaking compared with otherwise motivated offenses. And, when considering the physical injuries suffered by victims of hate crimes and parallel crimes as reported in the Crime Survey for England and Wales, the evidence seems to run counter to the accepted wisdom about the excessive brutality in hate crimes:

- Victims in incidents of violent crime perceived to be 'hate motivated' were less likely to report being injured than to report suffering no injury, whereas in incidents of otherwise motivated violent crime, victims were more likely to report suffering injury than no injury.
- There were also higher proportions of victims in incidents of wounding and assault with injury for otherwise motivated crimes than in 'hate crimes.'
- Over half of victims in incidents of otherwise motivated crime reported that they suffered severe bruising, minor bruising, a black eye, scratches, or cuts, compared with only two out of five victims in incidents perceived to be hate motivated.

For such findings to be conclusive, further analyses need to be conducted over time and in different countries to determine whether the evidence can be replicated. However, as it stands, the evidence seems to suggest that globally, hate violence is more likely to be excessively brutal in episodes of mass violence and less so in more socially secure conditions.

Hate crimes may possibly have become less violent since the period of the early 1990s when Levin and McDevitt collected their data from the Boston police. In the United States, the rate of murder—and especially the rate of murder committed by juveniles—had peaked between 1986 and 1992. By the mid-1990s, the rate of violent crime including offenses committed by youths had begun to plummet. Prevention programs as well as law and order policies were effective in fighting crime in general and violence committed by young people in particular. Specifically, American cities where juvenile violence had exploded enacted programs to supervise youngsters who would otherwise have been on their own when the school bell rang and they were dismissed. There was a dramatic increase in after-school athletic programs, teen centers, skating rinks, public swimming pools, summer jobs programs, and the like. More police officers were assigned to crime hot spots. Local community residents—clergy, teachers, parents, probation officers, parole officers, police, business leaders, and college students—collaborated in a vast community partnership to reach out to young gang members and other potentially violent youths. Violent hate crimes perpetrated by teenagers and young adults generally seem to have declined for the same reasons that youth violence has decreased.

Over the same period, many police departments in the United States have included the prevention of and response to hate crime in their training programs. Moreover, hate crimes committed by young people are no longer treated widely as mere childish pranks. Indeed, there is some evidence to indicate that few teenaged hate crime offenders receive a proverbial slap on the wrist from the criminal justice system. Teenaged perpetrators are more likely than their adult counterparts to be the recipients of alternative sentencing, but few youngsters get a sentence of unconditional probation. Most are required to do community service or engage in victim restitution. As punishment for some hate-motivated crimes—murder and vandalism—teens receive longer prison sentences than do adult offenders for the same crimes (Levin et al. 2007).

Physical Consequences of Violence against Women

While the proverbial jury might still be out on the matter of whether hate crimes in socially stable nations are excessively brutal, there are some evident distinct particularities of hate violence when the evidence of violence against women is considered. The first-ever survey of violence against women across the 28 member states of the European Union (FRA 2014), referred to in the last chapter, showed that when asked about the most serious incident of physical violence they had experienced since the age of 15, victims of partner violence were more likely than victims of non-partner violence to report that the most serious incident resulted in injuries. They were also more likely to report several different types of injury. The same was the case for women who had experienced sexual violence. Suffering injury, and suffering several types of injury, was more likely to be reported by women in cases of sexual violence by a partner (FRA 2014: 58–59).

When the problem of violence against women is considered globally, there are particular physical consequences of intimate partner violence which distinguish violence against women from other forms of hate violence. This is the case not only in zones of conflict, but also in rather more stable social conditions. Studies from Africa and India (WHO 2013) show that, for women, intimate partner violence is associated with increased risk of contracting HIV and other sexually transmitted infections. This comes about through the behavior of men who engage in such violence and the dynamics of the violent relationship. Men who engage in violence against their intimate female partners are more likely than non-violent men to engage in HIV-risk behaviors, such as having multiple sexual partners, using sex workers, and frequently using alcohol. Women in violent relationships, in the face of controlling behavior from men, are less likely to exercise control over sexual intercourse. This raises the potential for such women to be directly infected through sexual intercourse that is consensual, coerced, or forced.

Adverse reproductive health outcomes also arise out of women's loss of control over contraception that can occur in violent relationships. The research evidence indicates that women in violent relationships are more likely to have unintended pregnancies and more likely to have an induced abortion. And when illegal and unsafe abortions are carried out, the health risks for the women involved are greater. The stress associated with living in an abusive and violent relationship also has an impact on maternal health. Intimate partner violence has been shown to be a significant risk factor for low-birth-weight babies and pre-term birth (WHO 2013).

The Emotional and Psychological Consequences of Hate Violence

In the last chapter in discussing the long-term mental health trauma suffered by women survivors of systematic mass rapes during the 1992–95 war in Croatia and Bosnia and Herzegovina, we illustrated how studies of sexual violence used for 'ethnic cleansing' in conflict zones indicate profound damaging impact. Beyond regions of conflict in rather more secure social conditions, studies in the United States and the United Kingdom of the emotional and psychological consequences of hate violence clearly show that such violence hurts more than other forms of violence. Victims of hate violence are more likely to experience post-victimization emotional and psychological trauma than victims of other types of violence. While the pattern of difference is not consistent for every single victim, on average, when the emotional and psychological injuries are measured, it is clear that hate violence hurts more than other types of violence do.

A number of key themes of evidence stand out from the research to date:

- Victims in incidents of hate violence are more likely to report having an emotional or a psychological reaction to the incident and with a greater intensity, compared with victims of otherwise motivated violence (Iganski & Lagou 2014).
- For specific symptoms of emotional and psychological trauma, victims of hate violence are more likely to report experiencing anger, anxiety, crying and tears, depression, difficulty concentrating, fear, loss of confidence, nervousness, reduced feelings of safety, sleep difficulties, and withdrawal (Iganski & Lagou 2014).

- Interviews with victims of hate violence indicate that the aftermath of the victimization is characterized by a pervasive feeling of fear. Their fear may be based on threats by the offender or friends of the offender but often it is simply based on the random nature of the crime (McDevitt et al. 2001).
- Differences in reported post-victimization emotional and psychological impact between victims of hate violence as a group and victims of other types of violence holds when controlling for differences in the type of crime experienced (Botcherby et al. 2011; Iganski & Lagou 2014).

The emotional and psychological impact of hate violence has also been illuminated in greater depth than can be achieved by survey research, but with necessarily smaller and generally purposive samples, through a number of qualitative studies which have focused solely on hate crime victims without comparison samples of victims of parallel crimes. A small qualitative study of hate crime victims in Latvia published by the Latvian Center for Human Rights drew out, in depth, the profound and long-lasting psychological impact that can be inflicted (Dzelme 2008). Participants in the research reported that the psychological trauma suffered by victims of hate violence surpassed any immediate physical injuries that were inflicted. Some victims felt that it was the very essence of their being that was attacked.

But at the same time, because it is the victim's group identity that is attacked, hate crimes are not personal. Because of this they convey the potential for repeat victimization. Consequently, some victims in the Latvian study said they felt powerless and a constant sense of insecurity and alertness to the potential for repeat attacks, marked by suspicion of others and constant assessment of their immediate surroundings with calculations of safety and danger. Such particular and unique reactions to hate crime occur because they are attacks upon the core of the victim's identity (Craig-Henderson & Sloan 2003). Hate crimes can be seen as 'message crimes,' conveying to the victim and those who share the victim's identity that they are devalued, unwelcome, denigrated, despised, and even hated. The victim carries around with them the reason for their victimization: their visible appearance and what it represents to others in the dominant culture. In order to avoid potential victimization, some, where possible, will try to modify their appearance to reduce their visibility by, for example, concealing religious symbols or not wearing cultural styles which mark them out as 'different.'

Repairing the Harm of Hate Violence

As we have shown, hate violence inflicts particular harms and consequences upon victims and communities. When examined globally, it is clear that hate violence constitutes a serious global public health problem. We have also shown that the emotional and psychological impact of hate violence can be greater than the physical injuries inflicted. While hate violence accounts for more fatalities in areas of conflict than in relatively more stable social conditions, the emotional and psychological aftermath is likely to be profound wherever hate violence occurs.

Understanding the potential particular impact of hate violence, over and above the same types of crime which occur for other reasons, the need for effective support for victims is critical (FRA 2012: 20). Sensitivity and empathy in responding to victims of hate violence are essential given the particular emotional and psychological wounds that can be inflicted as discussed in this chapter. Non-governmental organizations (NGOs) and civil society organizations can play a key role in supporting victims of hate violence. Many of those who work for such organizations dedicated to supporting victims of hate crime have experienced hate violence themselves. Their specialist experiential expertise cannot be offered to the same extent by criminal justice agencies and other public authorities, as those tasked to manage hate crime would not generally have experienced it personally.

Despite the good work done by NGOs and civil society organizations in supporting victims of hate violence, there has been little sharing of good practice internationally and there is a great need to learn from initiatives around the world. And while the experiential dimension is valuable for the understanding necessary to support victims of hate violence, ideally, professionally skilled and systematic counseling interventions will also be necessary in many cases, especially those in which the post-victimization distress is acute. There will be two overriding goals for the counseling: first, ameliorating the victim's acute symptoms of post-victimization trauma, and second, addressing the critical challenge that can be posed by hate violence to the victim's in-group identity and their attitudes and behavior toward their victimizer's group (Dunbar 2001: 284–85). Repairing the harm of hate violence, therefore, is not only to the personal benefit of the victim but potentially to the benefit of many others too.

QUESTIONS FOR DISCUSSION

1. It what ways might it be concluded that hate crime inflicts a greater impact than otherwise motivated crime?
2. All violence hurts, but there is something distinctively hurtful about hate violence. What might that be?
3. How might healing the wounds of hate violence require more than attending to any physical injuries inflicted?

7:   A Typology of the Motives of Hate Crime Offenders

W hat are the impulses that drive hate crime offenders? Is a hate crime solely a matter of bigotry, bias or even hate? Or are other motives also at work? As discussed in previous chapters, while the background cultural edifice of prejudice provides a necessary condition for hate crime to occur, it is not a sufficient condition. Focusing on the background context leaves some fundamental questions unanswered. Chiefly, what is it that impels some people, but not others, to commit acts of hate violence? This is the question that we address in this chapter and the next.

In this chapter we revisit the widely cited typology of hate crime offending devised by Jack Levin and Jack McDevitt (1993; 2002) using hate crime reports from the Boston police in the early 1990s. One contribution made by the typology for understanding hate crime was that it dispelled the notion that hate crimes are generally committed by bigoted extremists, carrying out premeditated violent attacks for no other reason than targeting their hate. Instead, a number of different types of impulses were identified. We begin to unfold the typology with the largest single category identified by Levin and McDevitt, thrill hate crimes.

Thrill Hate Crime

On December 20, 2011, 20-year-old Taylor Giresiand and his 17-year-old companion—who lived together in Lake Como, New Jersey—filmed their vicious attack on a homeless man whom they repeatedly punched and kicked in the face and then dropped to the ground in the woods of nearby Wall Township. As posted on YouTube, the video showed the perpetrators having a good laugh as their victim held his bleeding face and struggled to escape. At the end of the episode, the younger assailant smiled at the camera, wished the homeless man "a merry Christmas," and then could be seen stealing his victim's bicycle.

The inspiration for thrill hate crimes depends on the state of a perpetrator's psychological needs. The sadism in such attacks is often an indicator that a desire to be powerful and in charge of things may be at the basis of an attack, at least on the part of the leader. Since the late 1990s, for example, state legislatures in seven states—Alaska, California, Florida, Maine, Maryland, Rhode Island, and

Washington—along with Puerto Rico and the District of Columbia, have broadened their hate crime protection to include homeless people who are frequently victimized for the fun of it by groups of young people. In some cases, the perpetrators have actually recorded their attacks on their smartphones. You can hear the offenders laugh out loud as they sadistically beat their homeless victims into submission with a baseball bat or their fists.

The manifest motivation for such thrill hate crimes is to gain a feeling of excitement. In the process, the perpetrators acquire symbolic capital in the form of bragging rights with their friends as well as a sense of superiority over their victim. In many thrill-oriented hate incidents, an influential member of the group who possesses a sadistic streak commits an assault or an act of vandalism against an individual that that member regards as subhuman or demonic. However, not every offender is necessarily a hatemonger. Instead, they may simply be fellow travelers who go along to get along, so to speak. Their primary objective is to maintain their position in the group as a valued and trustworthy friend. They therefore seek acceptance rather than superiority.

The character of thrill hate crimes reveals that hate attacks in the United States and Canada, and also elsewhere in the world, tend to be carried out by otherwise ordinary individuals. Offenders might be disaffected and disillusioned, but they usually do not belong to any organized hate groups. More likely, they hold a full-time job or attend classes at a local school or college, engage in a stable relationship with a partner, help their children with their homework, watch television, play popular videogames, or explore the internet. But on Saturday night, while their less hate-filled peers might get together to play a game of cards or go to the cinema, these dabblers in hate search with their companions for an appropriate victim to terrorize or bash.

Thrill hate crimes are not confined to the United States. In a particularly notorious episode in Russia in 2014 widely reported by the international news media, the neo-fascist group Occupy Pedophilia carried out violent homophobic attacks in a number of Russian cities in which they entrapped men looking for same-sex encounters and berated them with hateful homophobic invective. In a further act of humiliation of the victims, the group posted videos of the attacks on social networking websites. While the group was clearly on a violent 'mission' against gay men, the sadistic thrill they enjoyed was obvious from the video footage.

On occasion, incidents of the most brutal thrill murders are hate-motivated. As presented in Chapter 4, Jennifer Daugherty, an intellectually challenged resident of suburban Pittsburgh, was abducted by six of her "friends." The six assailants brought Daugherty to an apartment in Greensburg where they tortured her for 36 hours. They then forced Daugherty to write a suicide note and stabbed her to death. Finally, the six wrapped their victim's body in Christmas decorations and placed her in a garbage can, which they dumped in the parking lot of a local school.

Defensive Hate Crime

Unlike thrill-motivated incidents, defensive hate crimes are typically perpetrated by a single adult offender in the aftermath of some threatening event—a gay rights rally, a terrorist attack by Islamist extremists, a member of a minority group who achieves high political office, the first Asian resident who moves into a previously all-white neighborhood, or the like. From the standpoint of the perpetrator, their attack is neither exciting nor amusing. A group considered to be 'foreigners' has threatened the offender's physical survival, economic well-being, political advantage, or cultural/ religious values. In response, the perpetrator seeks to protect his interests or values by demonstrating that the foreigners do not belong in the neighborhood, the campus, the workplace, or the entire community.

Thrill-motivated hate crimes can occur at any time when the perpetrators are bored or idle. By contrast, defensive hate crimes against particular groups tend to peak when their presence represents a serious threat—either symbolic or real—to the perpetrator. In the United States, for several months following the 9/11 attack, there was a dramatic increase (1,600 percent, according to the FBI) in hate-motivated assaults committed against Muslim and Arab Americans. In similar fashion, racist hate-motivated attacks peaked in 2008, coinciding with President Obama's first-term election victory; homophobic hate assaults soared in 2003 at the same time that the first gay marriage law was passed by the state of Massachusetts; and hate-motivated attacks against Latinos peaked in 2010, at a time when the unemployment rate had not yet recovered from recession and the number of immigrants from Latin American countries had risen precipitously (Levin and Reichelmann, 2015).

Even in beauty pageants, when minority ethnic competitors have been crowned as beauty queens, some people feel their sense of national identity has been threatened, leading to defensive outbursts on social media. In 2013 Nina Davuluri, whose parents emigrated from India, was the first South Asian woman to be crowned Miss America. Abuse soon followed on Twitter. How representative of the US were these tweeters? Some tweets accused her of not being American, being an "Arab," and even looking like a terrorist. As one Twitter user wrote: "How the **** does a foreigner win Miss America? She is an Arab! #idiots." Another Tweeter wrote: "It's called Miss America. Get outta here New York you look like a terrorist. #bye#americanforamerica."

Again, this type of hate is not confined to the US. In 2013, the newly crowned Miss France was subject to racist abuse on Facebook and Twitter. Some of the posters referred to Flora Coquerel, whose mother is from the Republic of Benin in West Africa, as a "n*gger." One asked for "death to foreigners." Another asked: "I'm not a racist but shouldn't the Miss France contest only be open to White girls?"

When they occur at the neighborhood level, defensive hate crimes are frequently effective. They have been known to frighten victims into vacating their residence, their workplace, or their school in favor of an alternative location where they feel safe and comfortable. The influence of defensive hate crimes has apparently grown over the last few decades as more and more blacks, Latinos, Asians, and other ethnic minorities in the US have relocated from segregated residences into previously all-white neighborhoods. Racial segregation continues to hold sway in most housing markets in the United States, but it has also diminished significantly since the 1960s (Glaeser & Vigdor 2012).

Until recent years, for example, sections of Metairie, Louisiana, a middle-class suburb outside of the city of New Orleans, had remained all-white. Then, in May 2008, two US black American professionals, Travis and Kiyanna Smith, a 35-year-old chef and his 34-year-old cosmetologist wife, along with their three children, moved into the neighborhood. Only a few days later, they awoke to find the letters KKK (for Ku Klux Klan) and three crosses burned into their front lawn. Apparently, one or more of their neighbors were not terribly happy about the racial identity of the new residents on their block.

In the Metairie case, however, the Smith family refused to relocate. Moreover, they left the symbols of hate displayed on their lawn, hoping that all of the residents of their community would view them and be repulsed. Almost two months later, on Independence Day (July 4th), hundreds of people, both black and white, including friends, neighbors, religious leaders, and other concerned citizens gathered at the northeast Metairie home of the Smiths to hold an inter-faith service and to obliterate the racist symbols in their front lawn. Participants took turns digging up and re-sodding the defaced area of grass. More importantly, they sent a message of goodwill and respect to the members of the Smith family who, for the first time since moving, felt entirely at home.

Racism is only one of the differences that can form the motivation for committing a defensive hate crime. In April, 2014, Edmond Aviv, a 62-year-old resident of South Euclid, Ohio, was convicted of harassing his next-door neighbor, Sandra Prugh, and the members of her family. Prugh's husband has dementia, and her three children have disabilities—cerebral palsy, epilepsy, and a paralyzing illness. Over the course of the last 15 years, Aviv had spit on Prugh several times, repeatedly lobbed dog feces on her son's car windshield, and smeared feces on the Prugh family's wheelchair ramp.

In response, a local judge ordered Aviv to serve 15 days in jail, undergo anger management classes and counseling, send a letter of apology to Sandra Prugh, and stand on a street corner for five hours, holding a sign that read:

I am a bully! I pick on children that are disabled, and I am intolerant of those that are different from myself. My actions do not reflect an appreciation for the diverse South Euclid community that I live in.

Certain defensive hate crimes can be regarded as retaliatory. They are set off by the perception, correct or not, that a violent or unjust act has been directed against members of their group—that they are the victims. As a result, the victim becomes the villain, playing a game of tit for tat that can easily escalate into full-blown inter-group conflict and terrorism or mass murder.

Retaliatory Hate Crime

In a retaliatory hate crime, the actual perpetrator of the initial attack is typically not a target of violence. Instead, members of the victimized group direct their hatred randomly, causing acts of terrorism to be committed indiscriminately in what can become a vicious cycle of warfare.

In the United States, certain retaliatory hate crimes have developed out of the psychopathology of the perpetrator. The first week of May 2014 was a particularly bloody time in Isla Vista, California. Near the campus of the University of California at Santa Barbara, six students were shot to death by Elliot Rodger, the 22-year-old son of a Chinese American and a European American, who blamed everybody but himself—and females on campus, in particular—for his inability to attract women.

Hate-motivated massacres in the United States tend to be motivated by the killer's need for revenge. The killer fits a profile. He may be chronically depressed and unable to cope with the frustrations of everyday life; he is socially isolated, externalizes responsibility, and has access to and training in the use of firearms. Having never been hospitalized as a danger to himself or others, Rodger was able to secure his semi-automatic handgun legally. Not unlike most other rampage killers, he planned his attack for at least a year.

The feelings of shame that accumulate in an individual whose self-esteem is habitually low can provoke intense anger and a need to retaliate. Depending on circumstances, the target group might consist of family members, co-workers, classmates, all members of a particular group, or all of humanity. Rodger had complained bitterly about being bullied during his earlier years in school, being a virgin at the age of 22, and being rejected by one girl after another during his teenage years. Eventually, he came to blame women for all of his miseries in life. Based on the psychiatric profile we have of him, he seemed to be a sociopath and not simply a revenge killer.

Acts of terrorism can also involve retaliatory hate. Brothers Tamerlan (26) and Dzhokhar (19) Tsarnaev, who in April 2013 planted deadly explosives at the finish line of the Boston Marathon, apparently came to identify closely with the cause of radical Islam, but that is not the whole story. These marathon terrorists were more like rampage killers who enter a school, cinema, or shopping mall and indiscriminately target anything that moves. Their motive for planting explosives near the finish line of the marathon seemed to be revenge. They apparently held the United States responsible for wars in Afghanistan and Iraq. But they also seemed to blame Americans in general for their personal miseries.

It has been reported that Tamerlan was intensely angry—so much so that he disrupted a prayer service at his local mosque (Martinez 2013). The brothers' uncle referred to the two terrorists as "a couple of losers." And it was true that Tamerlan had recently suffered some major losses. He had become unemployed, was on welfare, and was dependent on his wife's meager income. Moreover, the older brother claimed to have had no American friends. The "final straw" may have occurred when Tamerlan, who was reputedly the best boxer in New England, was declared ineligible for national competition because of his lack of US citizenship.

Referring to the Boston Marathon bombing, President Obama used the term "self-radicalizing" to indicate the absence of an organized network such as al-Qaeda. In fact, many terrorists are no longer affiliated with organizations, even if they receive inspiration from them. Twenty years ago, the Federal Bureau of Investigation (FBI) was better able to infiltrate terrorist groups; nowadays, this has become—in cases where the terrorists are lone wolves or consist of a small "cell"—all but impossible. Since 9/11, the FBI has averted several potential acts of terror by their sting operations. On occasion, however, this tactic will probably be ineffective and the terrorists will succeed.

Undoubtedly, the most deadly retaliatory act of hate-motivated violence in the United States was perpetrated on September 11, 2001, when anti-American extremists flew commercial jets into New York City's World Trade Center, the Pentagon in Washington, D.C., and the ground of rural Pennsylvania. Almost 3,000 individuals, both on the ground and passengers in the three planes, lost their lives.

Some retaliatory hate crimes are very clearly politically motivated. The killer(s) have a cause. They seek to change national policy regarding immigrants, Americans, foreigners, Jews, Israel, Palestinians, or Muslims. The killing spree is designed to send a message of hate not only to each and every member of the victim's group but also to like-minded compatriots. He seeks to emphasize through violence that 'outsiders' simply will not be tolerated in his country.

In 2012, a mass shooting occurred outside of a Jewish school in Toulouse, France, where a lone gunman took the lives of a rabbi and three young children. Earlier in the same week, three French paratroopers, all either Arab or black, were shot to death in another terrorist attack. The message sent by the perpetrators was loud, clear, and deadly: Jews, Muslims, and other minorities are not welcome in our country. If you are Jewish, Islamic, or black, go back to your home country or you will be the next victim of violence.

Mission Hate Crime

In the United States, relatively few hate crimes are committed by the members of organized hate groups (Levin & McDevitt 1993). When such mission offenses occur, they tend to be particularly serious violent attacks such as aggravated assault or murder.

Mission hate crimes are committed by dedicated hatemongers who are willing to devote their lives to the cause of ridding the world of evil—the evil they associate with various groups considered to be outside of the mainstream. These hatemongers do not specialize. They think of Jews as the children of Satan, blacks and Latinos as "mud people," people with intellectual disabilities as "retards," and gays as pedophiles and deviants. They often make a career of expressing their hatreds, joining an organizing hate group, attending meetings on a regular basis, rehearsing for the revolution with their AR-15s and AK-47s on Sunday afternoons, and even committing acts of extreme violence.

In August 2012, 41-year-old Wade Michael Page shot to death six members of a Sikh Indian temple in Oak Creek, Wisconsin. He then took his own life by shooting himself in the head. Since 2000, Page had been a member of several neo-Nazi white power bands including End Apathy and Definite Hate. He apparently spoke frequently about an impending racial holy war and wore a number of white supremacist tattoos on his arms and upper body. Page was reportedly a member of the Hammerskins.

In April 2014, just prior to the Jewish holiday of Passover, 73-year-old Frazier Glenn Miller opened fire at two Jewish facilities—a Jewish community center and a retirement home—outside of Kansas City, taking the lives of three people (who ironically were not Jewish but Christian). According to the **Southern Poverty Law Center**, a civil rights organization out of Montgomery, Alabama, founded in 1971 to monitor, publicize, and resist the activities of right-wing hate groups in the United States, Cross was a longtime white supremacist and Grand Dragon of the Carolina Knights of the Ku Klux Klan, whose history originated shortly after the end of the Civil War in Pulaski, Tennessee, where a number of former confederate soldiers came together to form an organization dedicated to counteracting the growing political power of newly freed slaves. Miller has been charged in Johnson County, Kansas with one count of capital murder for the two slayings at the community center and one count of first-degree murder for the single slaying at the retirement community.

Fewer than 5 percent of all hate crimes are directly attributable to the members of organized hate groups, but their influence is vastly greater than their small numbers might indicate. Thanks to the internet, lonely and hate-filled youngsters can now log onto and visit hundreds of hate websites where they find interesting propaganda as well as chat rooms filled with like-minded hatemongers who are more than willing to engage in friendly and bigoted conversation. It takes few economic resources—a website, local access television, and voicemail—for an organized hate group to reach hundreds of thousands of disaffected and angry Americans and then to spread its venom around the world (Levin & McDevitt 1993, 2002).

There has been no shortage of mission offenders in Europe. Most recently in Greece in 2013–2014, where the spotlight has been shone on an apparent increase in racist violence in the context of the economic austerity and deprivations facing many Greeks, the **Racist Violence Recording Network** has noted that "Motorcycle or foot 'patrols' by people dressed in black" and acting "as self-proclaimed vigilante groups" have been implicated in attacks on migrants and refugees. In a small number of cases, some of the perpetrators have been noted to be wearing neo-Nazi style insignia of the far-right Golden Dawn party.

One hate-motivated murder was widely reported by the Greek and international news media. In the early hours of September 18, 2013, 34-year-old Pavlos Fyssas, anti-fascist hip-hop artist and concert promoter known as "Killah P," was stabbed in the chest twice and fatally wounded after leaving a bar in the Keratsini area of greater Athens. Fyssas was among a group of friends watching Champions League football on TV in the bar. After overhearing from the group a remark critical of the extreme-right Golden Dawn party, another customer allegedly phoned some Golden Dawn members to inform them of the presence of a traitor in his midst. A large group of men dressed in black T-shirts and combat trousers, many wielding weapons, descended on the area shortly afterward. Fyssas was surrounded by hatemongers and assaulted by an active member of Golden Dawn. Some witnesses alleged that motorbike policemen who had also arrived at the scene failed to intervene against the attack.

In Hungary, some particularly notorious attacks occurred in 2008 and 2009 when a small group dubbed by the media as the 'Death Squad' committed six racially motivated serial killings and numerous other attacks involving shootings and Molotov cocktails thrown at the houses of Roma. Four members of the Death Squad were arrested in August 2009. Following their trial, in which one member of the group stated that their aim was to intimidate the whole Hungarian Roma community, three of them were sentenced in 2013 to life imprisonment without the chance of parole, and the fourth to thirteen years in a maximum-security prison. While violence and discrimination against the Roma in Hungary has been a longstanding problem, the Death Squad murders occurred in the midst of a deepening economic crisis, in the context of the global financial crisis, with rising unemployment and growing nationalism, as we noted in Chapter 2.

The 'Ordinariness' of Hate Crime Offenders

Despite the evidence of extremism at work in the impulses behind mission hate crime, arguably the most telling observation that stands out from analyzing hate crime offenses is that most hate crime offenders are not 'extremists' who vent hate in premeditated violent attacks. Instead, many are otherwise 'ordinary people' who offend in the unfolding contexts of their everyday lives. Their actions are triggered by a variety of impulses and emotions (which we will discuss in the next chapter) not solely, and not often mostly, driven by 'hate.' Surprisingly perhaps, the same goes for extreme offenders. Pete Simi (2009), for instance, has shown how racist skinheads are more likely to be involved in opportunistic, situational, and spontaneous violence, often fueled by real or manufactured interpersonal disputes, whereby the targets are based on convenience, rather than carefully premeditated attacks in which they are acting out their bigotry with deliberation.

It would be too simplistic, therefore, to draw a hard distinction between 'extremists' and 'ordinary' people, as extremists have their very ordinary lives too (cf. Blazak 2009). This shows that offending does not define most hate crime offenders' lives. And hate crime offenders are not an aberration. In their actions, they express sentiments that are shared by others—as discussed across Chapters 2, 3, 4, and 5 of this book. Many people are sympathetic to the objectives of hardened hatemongers, but they also possess internal controls that keep them from expressing their sentiments in acts of violence.

Still, the Levin and McDevitt typology illustrated that prejudice, bias, bigotry, or hate, are often peripheral to the offender's impulses. This is captured very clearly in the category of 'thrill' hate crimes, whereby some offenders are mainly doing it for the laughs or for the buzz. This is a notion which might be difficult to accept at first because it might be taken to trivialize the offender's actions. It should be emphasized, therefore, that we are addressing the motivation for committing hate violence and *not* the consequences. The impact of hate crimes can never be regarded as trivial.

The typology also illustrated that in the United States, the overwhelming majority of hate crime offenders are dabblers who commit their hate crimes on a part-time basis as more of a hobby than a career. During the 1990s and prior to the 9/11 terrorist attacks, these dabblers in hate tended to be male teenagers and young adults who sought to counteract boredom by joining together with like-minded friends in order to attack a vulnerable victim—someone who was different with respect to race, religion, sexual orientation, gender, gender identity, or disability status. In the aftermath of 9/11, however, a larger number of hate-motivated attacks were defensive, being committed by older perpetrators and occurring when some event challenged the offender's privileged position in society. Hate violence became more of a way to fight back, even when a victim was selected randomly from an out-group and had absolutely nothing to do with the original threat.

QUESTIONS FOR DISCUSSION

1. In what ways does the Levin and McDevitt typology for understanding hate crime dispel the notion that such crimes are generally committed by extremists carrying out premeditated violent attacks for no other reason than targeting their hate?
2. What is the relationship between the background cultural context to hate violence and the different motivations and impulses behind offending?
3. Is there a difference between 'ordinary' and 'extremist' hate crime offenders?

8: Hate Violence and Emotion

What are the motivating impulses that drive hate crime offenders? That was the question that we began to address in the last chapter by discussing the Levin and McDevitt typology of hate crime offending. Informed by the typology, we noted that prejudice, bias, bigotry, or hate are often peripheral to the offender's impulses. In this chapter, we extend our analysis by focusing on the role that emotion plays in hate violence. We argue that emotion is one of the key drivers behind hate crime offending. There is an important body of scholarship on the significant role that emotion plays in the initiation and maintenance of violence in general. We build on this understanding by analyzing the role that human emotion plays in hate violence specifically. The point of departure for our analysis examines some critiques of the Levin and McDevitt typology.

Critiquing the Levin and McDevitt Typology of Hate Crime Offending

As well as being widely cited by scholars, the Levin and McDevitt typology of hate crime offending has featured prominently in law enforcement training materials in the United States and is featured on the National Institute of Justice Web site. The FBI's Training Academy in Quantico, Virginia, teaches this typology, and it was presented at the White House Conference on Hate Crimes opened by President Clinton in 1997.

The typology has also travelled widely internationally as it is used in hate crime training for national police departments in Bosnia and Herzegovina, Hungary, Poland, Northern Ireland, Croatia, the Ukraine, and the Czech Republic and the training of police officers from 59 countries who attend training conferences sponsored by the Office for Democratic Institutions and Human Rights in Europe. Overall, tens of thousands of police officers, prosecutors, and victim service providers have been trained to recognize offender motivations using the typology.

Despite the widespread impact of the Levin and McDevitt typology, Phyllis Gerstenfeld argued in her 2004 hate crimes text *Hate Crimes: Causes, Controls and Controversy*, that "its utility and meaning remain to be found" (2004: 77), implying perhaps that the typology still needed to be tested. Such a test was subsequently applied by Nickie D. Phillips (2009) in an analysis of court data from a New Jersey county.

Phillips' conclusion was that the Levin and McDevitt typology is "an inadequate tool for classifying cases prosecuted as hate crime" (2009: 883), noting that one-third of the bias crime cases she analyzed was "unclassifiable" according to typology (2009: 883). Phillips suggested that "the typology is useful for understanding cases in which the bias is the sole motivation, but inadequate for application to the many cases in which it is the peripheral motivation" (2009: 883).

To take Phillips' point, the Levin and McDevitt typology does categorize incidents where the bias, bigotry, prejudice, or hate is the primary or central motivating factor, although not the sole motivation. This is consistent with how hate crimes are generally conceived in the United States and elsewhere, such as in the Organization for Security and Co-operation in Europe's (OSCE) Office for Democratic Institution's (ODIHR) definition as discussed in Chapter 1 of this book.

Nevertheless, there are instances when the offender's bias is a peripheral or 'also ran' factor aggravating something else going on. Phillips reports that more than a third—eleven out of thirty—of the cases she analyzed were of this type and therefore did not fit any of the categories in the Levin and McDevitt typology. In these cases, bias did not seem to be the primary motivation. Instead the bias surfaced during the course of a confrontation whereby, according to Phillips, hate speech, which became the indicator for a hate crime, seemed to be used "as a means of expressing anger or other emotions in an arguably impulsive manner." To Phillips, these incidents often appeared retaliatory, but they did not seem to fit Levin & McDevitt's conceptualization of 'retaliatory hate crime' (Phillips 2009: 902).

While caution needs to be exercised in interpreting this finding as Phillips' study only included thirty cases prosecuted as bias crimes—far too low a number to draw any general inferences—her observation about the sometimes peripheral role of 'hate' in so-called 'hate crimes' chimes with other research findings (Phillips 2009: 895). Whether hate-aggravated criminal behavior is enough to establish an attack on a victim as a hate-motivated offense legally varies from country to country. In the United States, prosecution of a hate crime depends in part on confirming that a defendant's major motivation comes from the difference between offender and victim. By contrast, hate can legitimately be regarded as an aggravating factor in crimes committed in the United Kingdom and elsewhere in Europe.

Research conducted with London's Metropolitan Police Service researchers at **New Scotland Yard** from 2003 to 2005, and published in the book *Hate Crimes Against London's Jews* (Iganski et al. 2005), indicated that in a number of instances of the anti-Jewish crimes analyzed, the primary motivation of the offenders was not prejudice, bias, bigotry, or hate against Jews. Instead, hateful anti-Jewish invective was hurled during the course of an interpersonal conflict by a person (who by so doing became an offender) aggravating the situation with another person who in the process became a 'victim.' These incidents were categorized in the research as 'aggravated' hate crimes, and they accounted for about one in seven, or 14 percent, of a sample of 159 case records analyzed (Iganski et al. 2005). Following publication of that study, the category of 'aggravated' anti-Jewish crime has been used in the UK in the annual reports of the Community Security Trust (CST), an organization which advises and represents Britain's Jewish communities on matters of antisemitism, terrorism, and security—similar to the Anti-Defamation League in the United States.

The CST takes reports from victims who prefer not to go to the police in the first instance. It has been producing an annual count of antisemitic incidents reported to them since long before police forces in the UK began recording a separate category of antisemitic hate crime. For the 529 incidents recorded by the CST for 2013, they classified 12 percent as 'aggravated.' In one such incident which occurred in Manchester, according to the CST report, "A Jewish family were having a party and called a taxi to take home some of their guests. When it arrived, there was an argument over how many people could fit into the taxi and during the argument the driver said, "F**k off you Jewish b***h' and 'F**k off Jewish.' before driving off without any passengers." In another incident also in Manchester, according to the CST report "a visibly Jewish man was waiting to cross a junction in his car when a cyclist approached and, finding the man's car blocking his way, opened the car door, shouted 'b*****d Jew' and 'Jewish s**thouse' and spat in the Jewish man's face."

Hate Crime and Emotion

In the incidents just described and many more like them—some illustrated by Phillips (2009)—the person in the conflict situation who became the offender arguably suffered what psychoanalysts call a 'narcissistic injury' (Gilligan 2003: 1155), or in street vernacular they felt 'dissed'—in other words, disrespected. Some other words that might be used to describe the perceived injury include being slighted, insulted, demeaned, 'losing face'—all perceived rejections. In the circumstances of these incidents, the outburst of hateful invective might be seen as the offender righting the wrong they felt, restoring equilibrium by retaliating and inflicting a narcissistic injury in return (and in some cases also a physical injury), or cancelling out the shame they felt from the rejection. Much of this process is instinctive in that it occurs beyond conscious cognition.

Hate crimes are no different from other acts of violence in the emotional process that ensues. For instance, a study of the initiation, process, and escalation of physical conflicts and fights in Medellin, Columbia, involving 373 research participants between the ages of 15 and 24 recruited from the most impoverished and violent neighborhoods in the city, showed that insults or derogatory comments provided the trigger for violence in over half of cases, followed by "someone harassing a person's friend or companion" in another quarter of cases (Duque & Montoya 2013).

A common denominator in these types of incidents—whether a 'hate crime' or otherwise—is that the offenders often feel they have been wronged or slighted in some way and retaliate to impose an informal instance of justice on the victim and repair the damage to the respect that the offender feels. The offenders' retaliation might be regarded from their point of view as cancelling out the wrong they felt they had suffered by inflicting the same hurt or a greater hurt than they felt. Hurting back is a common defense against the pain and suffering that have been felt. Even if the retaliation is verbal rather than physical, the words expressed are intended to wound. Perceived weak points are picked on. Such 'weak points' are socially constructed, and social constructions of difference, with negative connotations attached to some differences—skin color, ethnicity, religion, disability, sexuality, age, gender, body shape, or social class, for example—provide well-known 'weak points.' They are well-known because arguably they are lying in the minds of many, and for some people they might even be present in everyday discourse.

The feelings of hurt felt by the person who becomes the offender in the interaction may not solely be generated by the immediate conflict in which they are involved. Past hurts, or emotional 'baggage.' to put it colloquially, might compound the pain of the particular incident as raw nerves are scratched. The retaliatory outburst might then also be targeted well beyond the person inflicting the hurt in the immediate moment to past moments of hurt as well to impose an informal justice and right the wrongs of the past—again, such a process will commonly occur beneath the surface of the offender's conscious cognition. In addition to compounding incidents, offender 'baggage' may also be complicit in the emergence or the occurrence of the initial incident as the person who becomes the offender is over-, or even hyper-, sensitive to slights. While the expressed animus has an instrumental purpose in that it is intended to hurt back, arguably many offenders would not anticipate the full extent of the hurt they inflict, especially if it is words that are doing the wounding.

Shame is an emotion that appears to be fundamental to this process. The role of shame in precipitating violence was theorized almost 20 years ago by Herbert Thomas (1995) in the *Bulletin of the American Academy of Psychiatry and the Law*. Thomas proposed that when one is rejected (or 'dissed'), by others, feelings of shame are a natural or "primitive" response (Thomas 1995: 587). The intensity and pain of the shame response felt will vary from one person to the next. When the felt pain is intense it may be projected outward onto the person who inflicted the rejection and pain, against others possibly, or inward toward oneself. Vulnerability to a shame reaction will depend upon a number of variables. Vulnerability will be magnified when what is rejected is what the person rejects him- or herself—when a raw nerve is struck.

A key defense against shame is what might be called 'narcissistic resources': a sense of self-worth, pride, self-satisfaction, a sense of being valued, a sense of importance, as attained through culturally constructive ways such as work, education, artistic endeavor, sport, material acquisition, family, and relationships. For some people, though, the means of attaining these resources are frustrated and even denied. With few other means at their disposal, violence, consciously or not, becomes a resource for some people for attaining and maintaining respect, dignity, and self-worth. Such persons will be hyper-sensitive to infringements, transgressions, or disrespect. Once their sense of self is challenged, violence might be their only resource for rebuilding and protecting it.

People with high self-esteem can better manage shame; they have had sufficient experience with pride to outweigh their experience of shame. However, when a person has had an insufficient accumulation of pride, then shame can become a calamity for them. When they experience some form of humiliation, real or imagined, rather than acknowledging it, it is masked with anger. The person is then caught in a 'shame-rage feeling trap' (Scheff et al. 1989: 185). According to Thomas Scheff and colleagues who have theorized this relationship between shame and violence:

> . . . rage is used as a defense against threat to self, that is, feeling shame, a feeling of vulnerability of the whole self. Anger can be a protective measure to guard against shame, which is experienced as an attack on the self. As humiliation increases, rage and hostility increase proportionally to defend against loss of self-esteem.
>
> (Scheff et al. 1989: 184)

Arguably, such understanding begins to address the question of why it is that particular people act in a certain way at certain times by committing acts of hate crime while others who find themselves in the same circumstances do not.

Emotion and Everyday Hate Crime

We have proposed in this chapter that emotion is one of the key drivers behind hate crime offending. As we noted in the last chapter, many offenders are just 'ordinary people' who offend in the unfolding contexts of their everyday lives. In this chapter we have focused on particular occasions when such contexts become highly emotionally charged, when everyday interpersonal disputes or conflicts arise and bias surfaces during the encounter. In such situations some of the parties to the conflicts pick on socially constructed 'weak points' to abuse those who they feel have disrespect or wronged them. As we have noted in this chapter, such weak points involve negative social constructions of difference commonly relating to skin color, ethnicity, religion, disability, sexuality, age, and gender, and even body shape, and social class. When physical violence ensues, it can become aggravated by such abuse. Such understanding takes us some steps in disentangling the connections between the background cultures of bigotry and prejudice which inform hate violence and the foreground of individual acts of hate crime.

QUESTIONS FOR DISCUSSION

1. What are the differences between 'hate' being a motivating or an aggravating factor for hate crime?
2. When considering offenders' emotions, in what ways might hate violence be understood as retaliatory violence?
3. What role might shame play in the impulses behind some hate crime offending?

9: Changing Cultures
Challenging Hate

~~~✵~~~

Highlighting the cultural contexts which spawn hate violence provides a major theme of this book. As we have argued throughout, hate violence is nested in cultures of bigotry, prejudice, stereotypes, and narratives about difference—real or imagined. Challenging hate violence therefore necessitates challenging cultural values. In this concluding chapter we focus on two very different types of intervention—legal and social—with the same aim of changing the cultures underpinning hate violence.

Hate Violence, Culture, and the Law

Hate crimes are 'message crimes.' Intentionally or not, perpetrators send a message that their target is disparaged, denigrated, and marginal. The message is not personal. It is not about the particular individual on the receiving end. It is about their identity and what that represents in the particular cultures in which hate violence occurs. Such representations give permission for violence.

Defining culture is not an easy task. There are many views on the matter, but little consensus. Along with many others, we share the view that culture is not simply about the arts, customs, or rituals of a society or a social group. Culture consists of acts of communication between human beings which give meaning to human existence and create the interpreted reality of experience.

In the context of the cultural foundations of hate violence, the communicative function of the law cannot be understated. It sends a message back that hate violence is abhorrent and beyond the bounds of civil conduct. Laws against hate crime are therefore a vital component of the counter-narrative against the cultural values which spawn hate violence. The target of the law is not only the everyday cultural values underpinning hate violence. Hate crime laws are also targeted at the cultures of criminal justice organizations—sending a message that hate violence must be taken seriously by representatives of law enforcement, the courts, probation, and the like.

Law and culture are deeply interwoven. The law is not simply an autonomous product of culture. The law is constitutive of culture (Geertz 1983) itself by providing a narrative of how a society seeks to visualize itself and envisions the relations between its members (Berman 2009). The law therefore not only sends a message of condemnation of hateful behavior: it *is* the message.

Using the law in this way to challenge culture does not impose a cultural straightjacket. In the case of hate violence, by seeking to restrain and alter aspects of culture that are destructive to human interaction, the law seeks to lay the foundations for the dynamic evolution of future social relations by denouncing the values that underpin hate violence and, by implication, promoting respect for diversity and difference. The law can provide encouragement and support in one or another direction—either toward the objective of maximizing segregation and hostility or toward the objective of maximizing peace and respect for differences.

The greater harms inflicted by hate crimes as discussed in Chapter 6 provide the justification for hate crime laws which impose greater penalties on convicted offenders compared with the penalties for similar but otherwise motivated crimes. Any objections that such laws impose restrictions on freedom of speech by punishing offenders for their expressed 'bad values' fail to acknowledge that the expressive evidence by which we come to recognize hate crime rarely consists of what we might conventionally call 'speech.' 'Invective' is a more accurate word.

However, while hate crime laws are an essential cultural force, it does not necessarily follow that all offenders should be subject to punitive measures upon conviction. The culpability of offenders is shared with the communities where the cultural values which spawn hate violence are prevalent. Many offenders who perhaps lash out in the heat of the moment in situations of heightened stress as discussed in Chapter 8, or who perhaps were having a laugh at the other person's expense or going along to impress friends, may not be aware of the full depth of hurt they inflict on their victim—the type of hurts discussed in Chapter 6. In many cases, rehabilitative interventions, or some other form of therapeutic intervention aimed at helping the offender begin to address the personal and social contexts for their offending will be more appropriate and just.

Recidivist hatemongers deserve to serve time behind bars. But when youthful first offenders commit hate crimes that are not of major proportions, the appropriate punishment may not be a lengthy prison sentence. Probation with rehabilitative conditions may be more effective. When the probationary mandate includes community service, victim restitution, and education, the sentence imposed by an enlightened judge and prosecutor can actually have the effect of transforming offenders from hate-filled miscreants into decent and respectful human beings who are eager to make amends for their hurtful behavior.

The Power of Interdependence

While hate crime laws are an important component of culture change, ultimately the reduction of hate violence depends upon persons modifying their attitudes and values. Social interventions can also be powerful in this regard. According to the contact theory of prejudice, increasing the interaction between groups tends to decrease the hostility between them. Of course, the quality of greater contact makes a big difference in determining its effectiveness. To work in a positive direction, the contact must involve a cooperative incident, receive institutional support, and include equal status groups (Allport 1954). When interaction lacks such characteristics, the level of hostility might remain intact or even worsen. Not all contact between groups reduces prejudice; sometimes, it only reinforces negative stereotypes.

Contact is most effective at promoting peace and harmony when the members of different groups are interdependent; that is, when they work cooperatively toward some kind of shared objective. In a classic study in social psychology, Muzifer and Carolyn Sherif (Sherif & Sherif 1961) established a summer camp for 11- and 12-year-old boys. At first, they separated the boys into two groups and placed them in different cabins. When the boys had developed a strong sense of group spirit and morale, Sherif and Sherif organized a number of competitive games including football, baseball, and tug-of-war—in which only one group could win (at the expense of the other). The result was clear-cut: competition produced negative inter-group feelings. The boys in each group began to name-call their opponents, totally turning against members of the opposing group, even against those whom they had selected as their best friends when first arriving at camp.

Then, to reduce the impact of competition on inter-group conflict, the researchers introduced a set of super-ordinate goals; that is, objectives that were shared by the members of both groups of campers. In order to achieve these common goals, the boys from both groups were forced to put aside their differences and become interdependent. For example, all of the boys piled into a bus in order to travel to a local town where an extremely attractive event was being held. Along the way, the Sherifs had secretly arranged to have the bus run off the side of the road and get stuck in the mud. At this point, the campers from both groups who were anxious to get to town had no choice but to work together as a team for the purpose of pushing the bus out of the mud. By their inter-group cooperation, the boys were able to achieve their super-ordinate goal of reaching the valued event in town. In the aftermath, they began again to develop friendships across group lines.

On many college campuses, influential students have initiated structured opportunities for interdependence by organizing coalitions of their schoolmates who come from diverse backgrounds but share the same objectives. Thus, undergraduates have organized the Jewish-Latino Coalition at the University of Texas, the Gay-Straight Alliance at Rowan University, the Coalition against Domestic Violence at the University of Delaware, and the Jewish-Muslim Coalition at UCLA, to mention only a few. College-based coalitions are formalized groups for promoting cooperation between groups. Actually, public schools and colleges represent one of the few institutions in society where such coalitions can be structured (Rabrenovic 2007).

We cannot afford to wait passively for interdependence to arise. Cooperation should be orchestrated rather than left to the vagaries of good fortune. In violence-prone areas around the world, interdependence has effectively brought opponents together despite the presence of ongoing warfare either within or between countries. Between 1969 and 2001, during the years of its considerable troubles, some 3,500 residents of Northern Ireland lost their lives to acts of terrorism and violent conflict. During this period, the country's Catholics and Protestants were separated in almost every aspect of everyday life. There were Protestant towns and Catholic towns, Protestant schools and Catholic schools, Protestant and Catholic bars, restaurants, and neighborhoods. Almost everything was segregated by religious identity; and when interaction occurred, it tended to be marked by conflict and violence.

Yet, at least one community in Northern Ireland was able to remain immunized against the sectarian segregation and violence that enveloped most other communities (Levin & Rabrenovic 2004). In this town, a shared infrastructure allowed the members of both religious denominations—Catholics and Protestants—to coexist. Local residents lived in integrated neighborhoods, and community members who operated businesses in town were engaged in mutually beneficial relationships across religious lines. The members of both religious groups shared local shops and offices, as well as pubs, clubs, and recreational facilities. The town's Protestants and Catholics participated in one another's christenings, marriages, and wakes. Interdependence existed in both an instrumental and an affective form. Local residents cooperated at work and in their neighborhoods.

Similarly, in the deeply entrenched hostilities involving Israelis versus Palestinians there have been important areas in which representatives from both sides of the conflict have come together in a spirit of cooperation (Levin & Rabrenovic 2004). In the Israeli settlement Kibbutz Metzer, Jews and Arabs were historically interdependent in a number of important areas of everyday life. Early on, the founders of Kibbutz Metzer were dependent on Arabs living in proximity to their collective farm for the basics of survival. For example, the settlement's Arab neighbors in Maisir Village shared with the Jewish settlers a pump for drawing water. In return, Kibbutz Metzer's nurse helped the Maisir villagers with health care. By 2002 the residents of both settlements were sharing a common water source.

Over the decades, friendship between the Jewish and Arab settlers gradually increased, along with their cooperative efforts at a more formal level. Palestinian children frequently visited the Kibbutz to play games and see the farm animals with their Jewish friends. Arab adults attended Jewish weddings and funerals. In politics, the members of Kibbutz Metzer strongly supported the establishment of a Palestinian state.

Even a horrible terrorist attack on the Jewish settlement could not extinguish the spirit of cooperation and friendship between Jewish and Arab neighbors. In November 2002 five residents of Kibbutz Metzer—including two young children and their mother—were gunned down and killed by a Palestinian terrorist. Rather than attempting to justify the violence, Arab residents of Maisir Village made condolence calls to the victims' families. They also lit candles and visited the scene of the tragic attack. Moreover, the Jewish settlers recognized the brutality of the deadly act of terrorism but never sought revenge. Instead, the murders only reinforced in the minds of Kibbutz residents the need to maintain cooperative relations with their Arab neighbors. The Palestinian members of Maisir Village agreed.

Another important example of the power of interdependence can be seen in the longstanding conflict between Hindus and Muslims in Kashmir, India, where thousands of people on both sides have lost their lives. The Muslim-Hindu divide widened considerably after Pakistan separated from India in 1947 and continued to grow into the 21st century. In August 2013, Hindu-Muslim violence spread throughout Kashmir, as more than 100 people were injured and at least six more were killed. After throwing rocks at a large crowd of Muslims as they marched from a mosque, local Hindus claimed they had been provoked by Muslim groups in the crowd who waved Pakistani flags and shouted pro-Pakistan slogans. Some evidence indicated that Muslim extremists then torched more than 100 Hindu-owned shops in retaliation (Nelson 2013).

Notwithstanding the long-term violence between Hindus and Muslims in Kashmir, Varshney (2002) was able to identify certain Indian localities in which residents resisted the pressure to engage in inter-group violence. In such peaceful communities, formal ties existed between residents who came from various ethnic or religious groups in order to pursue their shared goals. Local residents' common interests and public activities were promoted by a set of formal organizations that intervened between government and private family life. By contrast, such formal ties were absent from those communities in which inter-group violence occurred on a large scale. Where conflict erupted into violence, Hindus and Muslims lacked any significant inter-connections that might have brought them together in a spirit of cooperation and mutual benefit.

Varshney focuses on the town of Calicut, where Christian, Hindu, and Muslim residents lived in integrated communities connected by their joint participation in a variety of formal organizations such as business groups, labor unions, professional associations, and cultural organizations. Calicut's residents crossed religious lines to participate together in the activities of many civic associations such as trade unions, Lions and Rotary Clubs, and reading and art clubs. Informal ties also crosscut religious differences. In a survey conducted by Varshney, some 83 percent of Calicut's residents indicated that they ate with members of other religious groups in social situations, 90 percent indicated that their children played together, and 84 percent indicated that they visited each other regularly across religious lines. What began as cooperative relations in the formal sector became institutionalized at the informal level as well.

Interdependence usually does not arise out of thin air. It requires the ambitious support and encouragement of influential community members who recognize the value of cooperating between groups and are willing to organize their peers to that end. On many college campuses, there are more than a few students who have respect for differences and are capable of mobilizing others. These student leaders should be rewarded for their good work, but it rarely happens. Human beings seem to be very good at devising punishments for people who do the wrong thing; they are far less effective at rewarding people for their empathy and kindness.

QUESTIONS FOR DISCUSSION

1. In what ways are law and culture interwoven?
2. In what ways do hate crime laws involve cultural change?
3. What conditions appear to be necessary for interaction between groups to decrease the hostility between them?

References

Action Aid (2009) *Hate Crimes: The Rise of 'Corrective' Rape in South Africa*, London: Action Aid.

Allen, C. and Nielsen, J. S. (2002) *Summary Report on Islamophobia in the EU after 11 September 2001*, Vienna: European Monitoring Centre on Racism and Xenophobia.

Allport, G. (1954) *The Nature of Prejudice*, Reading, MA: Addison-Wesley.

Amnesty International (2004) *Lives Blown Apart: Crimes Against Women in Times of Conflict*, London: Amnesty International Publications.

Anti-Defamation League (ADL) (2014) *ADL Global 100: An Index of Anti-Semitism* (accessed January 19, 2015): http://global100.adl.org/public/ADL-Global-100-Executive-Summary.pdf

Barnett, V. J. (1999) *Bystanders: Conscience and Complicity during the Holocaust*, Westport, CT: Praeger.

Bennett-Smith, M. (2013) 'Gay teen allegedly stoned to death in Somalia for sodomy', *The Huffington Post*, March 21 (accessed January 19, 2015): http://www.huffingtonpost.com/2013/03/21/gay-teen-stoned-somalia-sodomy_n_2916655.html

Berman, P. S. (2009) 'The enduring connections between law and culture: Reviewing Lawrence Rosen, *Law as Culture*, and Oscar Chase, *Law, Culture, and Ritual*', *American Journal of Comparative Law*, 57: 101–111.

Blazak, R. (2009) 'Interview with a hate offender', in R. Blazak (ed.) *Hate Crimes Hate Crime Offenders* (pp. 189–205), Westport, CT: Praeger.

Botcherby, S., Glenn, F., Iganski, P., Jochelson, K., and Lagou, S. (2011) *Equality Groups' Perceptions and Experiences of Crime*, Manchester, England: Equality and Human Rights Commission.

Campbell, F. K. (2008) 'Exploring internalized ableism using critical race theory', *Disability & Society*, 23(2): 151–162.

Cohen, M. M., Forte, T., Du Mont, J., Hyman, I., and Romans, S. (2005) 'Intimate partner violence among Canadian women with activity limitations', *Journal of Epidemiology and Community Health*, 59(10): 834–839.

Commission on British Muslims and Islamophobia (2004) *Islamophobia: Issues, Challenges and Action*, Stoke-on-Trent, England: Trentham Books.

Connell, R. W. (1995) *Masculinities*, Berkeley: University of California Press.

Council of Europe (2013) *Report by Nils Muižnieks Commissioner for Human Rights of the Council of Europe following his visit to Greece from 28 January to 1 February 2013*,

Strasbourg: Council of Europe (accessed January 19, 2015): https://wcd.coe.int/View-Doc.jsp?id=2053611

Craig-Henderson, K. and Sloan, L. R. (2003). 'After the hate: Helping psychologists help victims of racist hate crime', *Clinical Psychology: Science and Practice*, 10(4): 481–490.

Dunbar, E. (2001) 'Counseling practices to ameliorate the effects of discrimination and hate events: Toward a systematic approach to assessment and intervention', *The Counselling Psychologist*, 29(2): 279–307.

Duque, L. F. and Montoya, N. E. (2013) 'From insult to injury: How disputes begin and escalate among adolescents and young adults in Medellin, Columbia', *International Journal of Criminology and Sociology*, 2: 169–179.

Dzelme, I. (2008) *Psychological Effects of Hate Crime*, Riga: Latvian Center for Human Rights.

European Commission against Racism and Intolerance (ECRI) (2013) *ECRI Report on the Russian Federation*, Strasbourg: Council of Europe.

European Commission against Racism and Intolerance (ECRI) (2014) *Annual Report on ECRI's Activities Covering the Period 1st January to 31st December 2013*, Strasbourg: Council of Europe.

European Union Agency for Fundamental Rights (FRA) (2009a) *Data in Focus Report: Muslims*, Vienna: Author.

European Union Agency for Fundamental Rights (FRA) (2009b) *EU MIDIS: Main Results Report*, Vienna: Author.

European Union Agency for Fundamental Rights (FRA) (2012) *Data in Focus Report: Minorities as Victims of Crime*, Vienna: European Union Agency for Fundamental Rights.

European Union Agency for Fundamental Rights (FRA) (2013a) *Discrimination and Hate Crime Against Jews in EU Member States: Experience and Perceptions of Antisemitism*, Vienna: European Union Agency for Fundamental Rights.

European Union Agency for Fundamental Rights (FRA) (2013b) *European Union Lesbian, Gay, Bisexual and Transgender Survey*. Vienna: European Union Agency for Fundamental Rights.

European Union Agency for Fundamental Rights (FRA) (2014) *Violence against Women: An EU-wide Survey—Main Results*, Vienna: European Union Agency for Fundamental Rights.

European Union Monitoring Centre on Racism and Xenophobia (EUMC) (2001) *Anti-Islamic Reactions in the EU After the Terrorist Acts Against the USA, Executive Summary*, Vienna: European Union Monitoring Centre on Racism and Xenophobia.

Feagin, J. R. and Vera, H. (1995) *White Racism,* New York: Routledge.

Geertz, C. (1983) *Local Knowledge: Further Essays in Interpretive Anthropology*, New York: Basic Books.

Gilligan, J. (2003) 'Shame, guilt and violence', *Social Research*, 70(4): 1149–1180.

Glaeser, E. and Vigdor, J. (2012) 'The end of the segregated century: Racial separation in America's neighborhoods, 1890–2010', (Civic report No. 66), Manhattan Institute (accessed January 19, 2015): http://www.manhattan-institute.org/html/cr_66.htm

Goodley, D. and Runswick-Cole, K. (2011) 'The violence of disablism', *Sociology of Health and Illness,* 33(4): 602–617.

Grare, F. (2007) 'The evolution of sectarian conflicts in Pakistan and the ever-changing face of Islamic violence', *South Asia: Journal of South Asian Studies*, 30(1): 127–143.

Harrell, E. (2014) 'Crime against persons with disabilities, 2009-2012: Statistical tables', *Department of Justice National Crime Victimization Survey* (February 25): 4.

Hassan, S. (2014) 'Understanding the dynamic of communal riots against Muslims in Muzaffarnagar and Shamli districts, Uttar Pradesh, India', in P. Grant (ed.) *State of the World's Minorities and Indigenous Peoples 2014* (pp. 121–124), London: Minority Rights Group International.

Haught, J. A. (1990) *Holy Horrors: An Illustrated History of Religious Murder and Madness*, Amherst, NY: Prometheus Books.

Herek, G.M. (1990) 'The context of anti-gay violence: Notes on cultural and psychological heterosexism', *Journal of Interpersonal Violence*, 5: 316–333.

Herek, G. M. (1992) 'The social context of hate crimes: Notes on cultural heterosexism', in G. M. Herek and K. T. Berrill (eds.) *Hate Crimes: Confronting Violence against Lesbians and Gay Men* (pp. 89–104), Thousand Oaks, CA: Sage.

Human Rights Watch (2011) *Sterilization of Women and Girls with Disabilities* (Briefing paper), New York: Human Rights Watch.

Human Rights Watch (2013) *'All You Can Do Is Pray': Crimes Against Humanity and Ethnic Cleansing of Rohingya Muslims in Burma's Arakan State*, New York: Human Rights Watch.

Iganski, P. (2011) *Racist Violence in Europe*, Brussels: European Network Against Racism.

Iganski, P., Kielinger, V. and Paterson, S. (2005) *Hate Crimes against London's Jews*, London: Institute for Jewish Policy Research.

Iganski, P. and Lagou, S. (2014) 'The personal injuries of "hate crime,"' in N. Hall, A. Corb, P. Giannasi and J. Grieve (eds.) *The Routledge International Handbook on Hate Crime* (pp. 34–46), London: Routledge.

Isaacs, T. (2001) 'Domestic violence and hate crimes: Acknowledging two levels of responsibility', *Criminal Justice Ethics*, 20(2): 31–43.

Itaborahy, L. P and Zhuriminali, J. (2014) *State Sponsored Homophobia*, Geneva: International Lesbian, Gay, Bisexual, Trans and Intersex Association (ILGA).

Juergensmeyer, M. (2003) *Terror in the Mind of God: The Global Rise of Religious Violence* (3rd ed.), Berkeley: University of California Press.

Katz, F. E. (1993), *Ordinary People and Extraordinary Evil*, Albany, NY: SUNY Press.

Kuruvila, M. C. and Lee, H. K. (2006). 'Religious hate seen as motive in killing', *SFGate*, October 20, http://www.sfgate.com/bayarea/article/Religious-hate-seen-as-motive-in-killing-2549569.php

Lattimer, M. (2014) 'Peoples under threat 2014: Hate crimes and mass killing', in P. Grant (ed.) *State of the World's Minorities and Indigenous Peoples 2014* (pp. 206–219), London: Minority Rights Group International.

Levin, J. (2013). 'Disablist violence in the US: Unacknowledged hate crime', in Roulstone and Mason-Bish1 (eds.) *Disability, Hate Crime and Violence* (pp. 95–105), London: Routledge.

Levin, J. and McDevitt, J. (1993) *Hate Crimes: The Rising Tide of Bigotry and Bloodshed*, New York: Plenum.

Levin, J. and McDevitt, J. (2002) *Hate Crimes Revisited*, Boulder, CO: Westview Press.

Levin, J. and Rabrenovic, G. (2004) *Why We Hate*, Amherst, NY: Prometheus Books.

Levin, J. and Reichelmann, A. (2015) 'From Thrill to Defensive Motivation: The Role of Group Threat in the Changing Nature of Hate-Motivated Assaults,' *American Behavioral Scientist*, in press.

Levin, J., Rabrenoviic, G., Ferraro, V., Doran, T. and Methe, D. (2007) 'When a crime committed by a teenager becomes a hate crime: Results from two studies', *American Behaviorial Scientist*, 51(2): 246–257.

Lin, L.-P., Yen, C.-F., Kuo, F.-Y., Wu, J.-L. and Lin, J.-D. (2009) 'Sexual assault of people with disabilities: Results of a 2002–2007 national report in Taiwan', *Research in Developmental Disabilities*, 30(5): 969–975.

Loch, A. A., Wang, Y-P., Guarniero, F. B., Lawson, F. L., Hengartner, M. P., Rössler, W. and Gattaz, W. F. (2014) 'Patterns of stigma toward schizophrenia among the general population: A latent profile analysis', *International Journal of Social Psychiatry*, 60(6): 595–605.

Lončar, M., Medved, V., Jovanović, N. and Hotujac, L. (2006) 'Psychological consequences of rape on women in 1991–1995 war in Croatia and Bosnia and Herzegovina', *Croatian Medical Journal*, 47: 67–75.

McDevitt, J., Balboni, J., Garcia, L. and Gu, J. (2001) 'Consequences for victims: A comparison of bias and non-bias motivated assaults', *American Behavioral Scientist*, 45(4): 697–713.

McFarqhuar, N. (1999) 'Eight are charged in tormenting of learning disabled man', *The New York Times* (February 17): 1.

Martinez, E. (2010) 'Jennifer Daugherty: "Friends" killed disabled woman, forced her to write suicide note', *CBS News* (February 12): www.cbsnews.com/2102-504083_162-6202062.html?tag=contentMain;contentBody

Martinez, M. (2013). 'Uncle calls Boston Marathon bombers "losers,"' *CNN.com* (April 19): http://www.christianpost.com/news/dzhozkar-tamerlan-tsarnaev-losers-says-uncle-ruslan-tsarni-boston-bomber-ask-for-forgiveness-video-94316/

Mason-Bish, H. (2015) 'Beyond the silo: Rethinking hate crime and intersectionality', in N. Hall, A. Corb, P. Giannasi and J.D.G. Grieve (eds.) *The Routledge International Handbook on Hate Crime* (pp. 24–33), Abingdon, UK: Routledge.

Matsuda, M. (1989) 'Public responses to racist speech: Considering the victim's story', *Michigan Law Review*, 87: 2320–2381.

Mihlar, F. (2014) ' "Everything Has Shattered"—Rising Levels of Violence against Shi'a in Pakistan' (Briefing), London: Minority Rights Group International.

Mind (2007) *Another Assault*, London: MIND.

National Coalition of Anti-Violence Programs (NCAVP) (2013) *Lesbian, Gay, Bisexual, Transgender, Queer and HIV-Affected Hate Violence in 2012*, New York: National Coalition of Anti-Violence Programs.

Nelson, D. (2013) 'Kashmir: Violence escalates between Hindus and Muslims', *The Telegraph*, August 11.

Nocon, A., Iganski, P. and Lagou, S. (2011) *Disabled People's Experiences and Concerns about Crime*, Manchester, England: Equality and Human Rights Commission.

Office for Democratic Institutions and Human Rights (ODIHR) (2009) *Hate Crime Laws: A Practical Guide*, Warsaw: OSCE/ODIHR.

Office for Democratic Institutions and Human Rights (ODIHR) (2013) *Hate Crimes in the OSCE Region: Incidents and Responses—Annual Report for 2012*, Warsaw: OSCE/ODIHR.

Perry, B. (2003) 'Anti-Muslim retaliatory violence following the 9/11 terrorist attacks', in B. Perry (ed.) *Hate and Bias Crime: A Reader* (pp. 183–201), New York: Routledge.

Pew Research Center (2013) *The Global Divide on Homosexuality*, Washington, DC: Pew Research Center.

Pew Research Center (2014) *Global Views on Morality*, Washington, DC: Pew Research Center.

Phillips, N. D. (2009) 'The prosecution of hate crimes: The limitations of the hate crime typology', *Journal of Interpersonal Violence*, 24(5): 883–905.

Rabrenovic, G. (2007). 'Responding to hate violence: New challenges and solutions', *American Behavioral Scientist*, 51(2): 143–148.

Rai, D. K. and Hesse, B. (1992) 'Racial victimization: An experiential analysis', in B. Hesse, D. K. Rai, C. Bennett and P. McGilchrist (eds.) *Beneath the Surface: Racial Harassment* (pp. 158–195), Aldershot, UK: Avebury.

Russian Analytical Digest (2013) 'Xenophobia and migrants', *Russian Analytical Digest*, 141: 8–12 (accessed January 19, 2015): http://www.css.ethz.ch/publications/DetailansichtPubDB_EN?rec_id=2828

Sandholtz, N., Langton, L. and Planty, M. (2013) *Hate Crime Victimization, 2002–2011*, Washington DC: US Department of Justice, Bureau of Justice Statistics.

Scheff, T. J., Retzinger, S. M. and Ryan, M. T. (1989) 'Crime, violence, and self-esteem: Review and proposals', in A. Mecca, N. J. Smelser and J. Vasconcellos (eds.) *The Social Importance of Self-Esteem* (pp. 165–199), Berkeley: University of California Press.

Schomerus, G., Schwahn, C., Holzinger, A., Corrigan, P. W., Grabe, H. J., Carta, M. G. and Angermeyer, M. C. (2012) 'Evolution of public attitudes about mental illness: A systematic review and meta-analysis', *Acta Psychiatrica Scandinavica*, 125(6): 440–452.

Sherif, M. and Sherif, C. (1961) *The Robbers Cave Experiment: Intergroup Conflicts and Cooperation*, Norman: University of Oklahoma Press.

Sibbitt, R. (1997) *The Perpetrators of Racial Harassment and Racial Violence* (Research study 176), London: Home Office.

Simi, P. (2009) 'Skinhead street violence', in R. Blazak (ed.) *Hate Crimes: Hate Crime Offenders* (pp. 157–170), Westport, CT: Praeger.

Smith, D. L. (2008) 'Disability, gender and intimate partner violence: Relationships from the behavioral risk factor surveillance system', *Sexuality and Disability*, 26(1): 15–28.

Sorsdahl, K. R. and Stein, D. J. (2010) 'Knowledge of and stigma associated with mental disorders in a South African community sample', *The Journal of Nervous and Mental Disease*, 198(10): 742–747.

South African Human Rights Commission (2008) *Report of the Public Hearing of School-based Violence*, Braamfontein, South Africa: South African Human Rights Commission.

Thomas, H. E. (1995) 'Experiencing a shame response as a precursor to violence', *Bulletin of the American Academy Psychiatry Law*, 23(4): 587–593.

Thomas, P. (2011) '"Mate crime": Ridicule, hostility and targeted attacks against disabled people', *Disability and Society*, 26(1): 107–111.

Turner, L., Whittle, S. and Combs, R. (2009) *Transphobic Hate Crime in the European Union*, Brussels: ILGA-Europe and Press for Change.

UK Home Office, Office for National Statistics (ONS), Ministry of Justice (MoJ) (2013) *An Overview of Hate Crime in England and Wales*, London: Home Office, Office for National Statistics, Ministry of Justice.

United Nations (2007) *From Exclusion to Equality: Realizing the Rights of Persons with Disabilities*, Geneva: United Nations.

United Nations Children's Fund (UNICEF) (1996) *The State of World's Children 1996*, Oxford: Oxford University Press.

United Nations High Commissioner for Human Rights (UNHCHR) (2011) *Discriminatory Laws and Practices and Acts of Violence against Individuals Based on Their Sexual Orientation and Gender Identity, A/HRC/19/41*, Geneva: United Nations Office of the High Commissioner for Human Rights.

United Nations High Commissioner for Refugees (UNHCR) (2014) *South East Asia—Irregular Maritime Movements*, Geneva: UNHCR Regional Office for South East Asia.

Varshney, A. (2002) *Ethnic Conflict and Civic Life*, New Haven, CT: Yale University Press.

Veldhuis, T. and Bakker, E. (2009) *Muslims in the Netherlands: Tensions and Violent Conflict*, MICROCON Policy Working Paper 6, Brighton: MICROCON.

Verma, J. S., Seth, L. and Subramanium, G. (2013) *Report of the Committee on Amendments to Criminal Law*, New Delhi: Committee on Amendments to Criminal Law.

Weisburd, S. and Levin, B. (1994) 'On the basis of sex', *Stanford Law and Policy Review*, 5(2): 21–47.

Welch, M. (2006) *Scapegoats of September 11th*, New Brunswick, NJ: Rutgers University Press.

Westie, F. R. (1964). 'Race and ethnic relations', in R.E.L. Faris (ed.) *Handbook of Modern Sociology*, Skokie, IL: Rand McNally.

Wilson, M. M. (2014) *Hate Crime Victimization, 2004–2012: Statistical Tables*, Washington, DC: Bureau of Justice Statistics, Office of Justice Programs.

Wolfe, K. (1995). 'Bashing the disabled: The new hate crime', *The Progressive* (November): 1.

World Health Organization (2011) *World Report on Disability*, Geneva: World Health Organization.

World Health Organization (2013) *Global and Regional Estimates of Violence against Women: Prevalence and Health Effects of Intimate Partner Violence and Non-partner Sexual Violence*, Geneva: World Health Organization.

Index

Note: Page numbers with *f* indicate figures.

Afghanistan 47
African states: intimate partner violence in
    29*f*, 39–40; mass killing and 2; same-sex
    sexual activities in 21
al-Qaeda 1; terror attacks 1; *see also* 9/11
    attacks
Al Shabab 21
Americablog 12
Anti-Defamation League 13–14, 54
anti-Muslim violence: continuing nature
    of 5; in Europe 4–5; extreme events
    triggering 5; in Western World 4–5
Antigua 20
antisemitism 12–14; Anti-Defamation
    League survey 13–14; in Europe 13*f*; in
    Hungary 12–13
Arakan State, Buddhists and Muslims
    sectarian violence in 3–4
Argentina 20
asylum seekers: in Greece 11; Myanmar
    violence and 4; as targets for extremists 15
Australia 20
Aviv, Edmond 46

Barbados 20
Barbuda 20
Belgium 20
Belize 20
Belarus 20
bias incidents, against persons 37*f*
Bolivia 20
Bosnia 26

Brazil 20, 26
brutality of hate violence 35–42; emotional/
    psychological consequences of 40–1; as
    excessively brutal 37–9; fatal hate violence
    36–7, 37*f*; overview of 35–6; repairing
    41–2; against women 39–40
*Bulletin of the American Academy of
    Psychiatry and the Law* (Thomas) 55

caliphate 2
Canada 20, 25, 44
Commission on British Muslims and
    Islamophobia 5
Community Security Trust (CST) 54
Coquerel, Flora 45
corrective rape 21
Council of Europe 10
Crime Survey for England and Wales 23–4, 38
Croatia 29, 52
Crusades 1
cultural context of hate violence, changing
    58–63; interdependence and 59–63; law
    and 58–9
culture, defining 58
Czech Republic 52

Daugherty, Jennifer 24, 44
Davuluri, Nina 45
Death Squad 50
defensive hate crime 45–7
derogatory language, as disablist violence
    24–5

disabilities, United Nations definition of 23
disablist 23
disablist violence 23–7; Crime Survey for
    England and Wales estimates of 23–4;
    cultural basis of 26–7; data on 23;
    overview of 23; reporting of 25; types of
    24–5; in United States 24
Dominica 20

Eastern Mediterranean countries, intimate
    partner violence in 29f
Egypt 19
El Salvador 20
emotion, hate violence and 52–6; explained
    54–6; Levin and McDevitt typology
    of 52–4; offender ordinariness and 56;
    overview of 52
emotional consequences of hate violence
    40–1
ethnic cleansing 29
EU Member States, violence against women
    survey 31–2, 32f
Europe: antisemitism in 13f; extremist
    violence in 10–12; intimate partner
    violence against women in 29f
European Commission Against Racism and
    Intolerance (ECRI) 10, 12; Council of
    Europe 10
European Union Agency for Fundamental
    Rights 5
European Union Minorities and
    Discrimination Survey (EU-MIDIS)
    9–10
extreme Islamist violence 2–3
extremist violence: in Europe 10–12;
    in Greece 10–11; in Hungary 11; in
    Russia 12

Facebook 12
fatal hate violence 36–7, 37f
FBI hate crime statistics 8, 9f
France 20
Fundamental Rights Agency (FRA),
    European Union: antisemitism and
    12–13; extremism in Europe and 10;

homophobic/transphobic violence and
    17; violence against women survey 31–2,
    32f; Western World violence against
    Muslims and 4–5
Fyssas, Pavlos 50

Gerstenfeld, Phyllis 52
Giresiand, Taylor 43
Golden Dawn Party 11, 49–50
Grenada 20
Grenadines 20
Greece: extremist violence in 10–11; Golden
    Dawn Party and 11, 49–50
Guyana 20
Gypsy criminality 11

hate crime xi; see also hate violence:
    cultural basis of xiii; described xi–xii; as
    message crime 41; Office for Democratic
    Institutions and Human Rights definition
    of xii; research and scholarship on xii;
    violence against women as 32–4
hate crime offenders, motives of 43–51;
    defensive hate crime 45–7; mission hate
    crime 48–50; ordinariness of 50–1;
    overview 43; retaliatory hate crime 47–8;
    thrill hate crime 43–4
Hate Crimes Against London's Jews (Iganski)
    53–4
Hate Crimes: Causes, Controls and
    Controversy (Gerstenfeld) 52
Hate Crimes: The Rising Tide of Bigotry and
    Bloodshed (Levin and McDevitt) 37–8
hate violence xi; see also individual headings:
    brutality of 35–42; cultural context
    of, changing 58–63; described xii–xiii;
    disablist 23–7; emotion and 52–6; as
    hate crime xi–xii; homophobic and
    transphobic 17–21; offenders, motives
    of 43–51; racial, ethnic, and xenophobic
    8–16; relationship between religion and
    6–7; religious 1–7; against women 28–34
hegemonic masculinity 33
Herek, Gregory 19
Herzegovina 29

heteronormativity, defined 21
heterosexism, defined 19
heterosexual masculinity 33
high-income countries, intimate partner
    violence against women in 29f
homophobic and transphobic violence
    17–21; cultural context of 18–21;
    overview of 17; scale of 17–18, 19f
homosexual acts, criminal law and 20
homosexuality, acceptability ranking of:
    in Asian/Pacific region 20; in European
    countries 20; in Latin American countries
    20; in Middle Eastern countries 19; in
    sub-Saharan African countries 20
Human Rights Watch 3, 25
Hungary: antisemitism in 12–13; Death
    Squad killings in 50; extremist violence
    in 11

Iceland 20
India 4, 6, 14, 30, 39, 62; communal
    violence in 4; interdependence in 62;
    violence against women in 30, 39–40
Indonesia 30
Inquisition 1
Instagram 12
inter-communal hatred 6
interdependence 59–63; in Calicut 62; on
    college campuses 60; in Kashmir, India
    62; in Kibbutz Metzer 61–2; in Northern
    Ireland 61; Sherif summer camp as 60
intimate partner violence, against women
    30–2; in African states 29f; in Eastern
    Mediterranean countries 29f; in Europe
    29f; G20 country rankings for 31f; in
    high-income countries 29f; physical
    consequences of 39–40; prevalence of
    28; in Southeast Asia 29f; in Western
    Pacific countries 29f; in young women's
    relationships 28
Iran 21
Iraq 35, 47
Islam denominations 2
Islamic caliphate, ISIS and 2
Islamic Jihads 1

Islamic State of Iraq and Syria (ISIS) 2
Islamophobia 4–5

Jamaica 20
jihads 1
jizya (protection tax) 2
Jordan 19

"Killah P" (Fyssas) 50
Ku Klux Klan 8, 49

Lashkar-e-Jhangri (LeJ) 3
Latvia 20; hate crime victims study in 41;
    spatial mobility in 14–15
Latvian Center for Human Rights 41
laws, against hate crime 58–9
Lebanon 19
lesbian, gay, bisexual, transgender and queer
    (LGBTQ) people 17; see also homophobic
    and transphobic violence; homicide risk
    for 18, 19f
Levin, Jack 37–8, 43, 51, 52–4
Lithuania 20
Luxembourg 20

masculinities, social construction of 33–4
mass killing rankings 1–2
mate crime 25
McDevitt, Jack 37–8, 43, 51, 52–4
message crime, hate crime as 41
Mexico 20, 30
Middle East states: homosexual acts in,
    penalties for 21; mass killing and 2
Miller, Frazier Glenn 49
Minority Rights Group International 1, 3
mission hate crime 48–50
Muslims: violence against, in Western World
    4–5; xenophobic hostility against 6–7
Myanmar, religious and sectarian violence
    in 3, 4

narcissistic injury 54
narcissistic resources 55–6
National Association for Mental Health
    24–5

National Coalition of Anti-Violence
    Programs (NCAVP) 18
National Crime Victimization Survey
    (NCVS) 9, 24
National Institute of Justice 52
Nevis 20
New Scotland Yard 53
New Zealand 20
Nigeria 21
9/11 attacks 48; Islamophobia and
    4–5
non-partner sexual violence, prevalence of,
    against women 28
Northeren Ireland 52
Norway 20

Occupy Pedophilia 12, 44
offenders *see* hate crime offenders, motives of
Office for Democratic Institutions and
    Human Rights (ODIHR) xii, 12, 18,
    23, 52
ordinariness, of hate crime offenders
    50–1, 56
Organization for Security and Co-operation
    in Europe (OSCE) 12; Office for
    Democratic Institution (ODIHR) 53

Page, Wade Michael 49
Pakistan 2, 3, 6, 62
Peoples under Threat index 1
perpetrator communities 16
Perry, B. 6
Pew Research Center 19
Phillips, Nickie D. 52–3, 54
Portugal 20
Prugh, Sandra 46
psychological consequences of hate violence
    40–1
psychological heterosexism 19

queer 17

racial, ethnic, and xenophobic violence
    8–16; antisemitism and violence against
    Jews 12–14, 13f; determinates of 15–16;

extremism, in Europe 10–12; history of
    8–10, 9f; spatial impact of 14–15
Racist Violence Recording Network
    49–50
rape, as weapon of war 29–30
Rwanda 35
religion and hate violence relationship 6–7
religious hatred 1–7; anti-Muslim violence,
    Western World 4–5; extreme Islamist
    violence 2–3; history of 1–2; religion/
    hate violence relationship 6–7; sectarian
    violence 3–4
retaliatory hate crime 47–8; Levin and
    McDevitt conceptualization of 53
Rigby, Lee (Corporal) 5
Rodger, Elliot 47
Roma/Gypsy communities, racist
    victimization in 10, 11
Russia 44; extremist violence in 12

St. Kitts 20
St. Lucia 20
St. Vincent 20
same-sex marriage 20
Saudi Arabia 21, 30
Scheff, Thomas 56
Scotland 20
sectarian 1; violence 1, 3–4; against Shi'a
    Muslims 3; in Syria 2; against Yazidi
    Christians 2–3
sectarian hatred 6
sexual violence against women: in public
    places 30; in regions of conflict 29–30
shame, violence and 55–6
shame-rage feeling trap 56
Sherif, Carolyn 60
Sherif, Muzifer 60
Shi'a Muslims, violence against 3, 6
silo approach to identity xiii
Simi, Pete 50
Sipah-e-Sahaba Pakistan (SSP) 3
skinheads 50–1
Smith, Kiyanna 46
Smith, Travis 46
social interventions 60

South Africa 20, 30
South African Human Rights Commission 21
Southeast Asia, intimate partner violence against women in 29*f*
Southern Poverty Law Center 49
Spain 20
spatial impact, of hate crime victimization 14–15
State of the World's Children (UNICEF) 29
Stormfront 25
Sunni militant groups 3
Sweden 20
Swift, Jonathan 6
Syria, mass oppression in 2

Taiwan 21
Tehrik-e-Taliban Pakistan (TTP) 3
theologically-driven hate 6
Thomas, Herbert 55
Thomson Reuters Foundation 30
Three Times the Violence (documentary film) 24
thrill hate crime 43–4
Tobago 20
transphobic violence 17–21; cultural context of 18–21; overview of 17; scale of 17–18, 19*f*
Trinidad 20
TrustLaw 30
Tsarnaev, Dzhokhar 47–8
Tsarnaev, Tamerlan 47–8
Tunisia 19
Turkey 19

Ukraine 20
Uniform Crime Reports (UCR) 8, 36
UNICEF 29
United Nations Commission for Human Rights 4
United Nations High Commissioner for Human Rights 18

United States: black Americans in 8; FBI hate crime statistics 8, 9*f*; LGBTQ and HIV-affected homicide victims in 19*f*; National Crime Victimization Survey (NCVS) 9; police-recorded crime data 8; racist violence in 8
Uruguay 20

van Gogh, Theo 5
Venezuela 20
violence against Jews *see* antisemitism
violence against women *see* women, hate violence against
Vkontakte 12

Wales 20
Western Pacific countries, intimate partner violence against women in 29*f*
Western World 4: anti-Muslim violence in 4–5; European Union hate crime estimates 9–10; racial, ethnic, and xenophobic violence in 8; religious animosity against Muslims in 6–7; United States hate crime estimates 8–9
White House Conference on Hate Crimes 52
women, hate violence against 28–34; conceptualizing, as hate crime 32–4; EU Member States survey of 31–2, 32*f*; forms of 29; G20 country rankings for 31*f*; global/regional estimates of 28–30, 29*f*, 31*f*; intimate partner violence 28–9, 29*f*, 30–2; overview of 28; physical consequences of 39–40; sexual, in regions of conflict 29–30
World Health Organization (WHO) 25, 28, 30

xenophobic 7; violence 7; in Russia 12

Yazidi 2; slaughter 2–3
Yemen 21